What others are saying about this book:

"...Of all the books I've read on Belize, and I've read plenty, the writings of Bill and Claire Gray are the only works I've found that are written by expatriates actually living in Belize. Their writing is a love affair with Belize. If you want to find out about living in Belize they are where we should start. Their books and their tours are simply the best."   *--Roger Gallo*
Author, Escape From America
President EscapeArtist.com website

"The Grays moved to Belize a few years ago, and are in a position to recount both the pros and cons of such a venture. Unlike tourist-oriented guides, this book blends basics on Belize's offerings with specifics on how to relocate to the country."   *--The Bookwatch*

"The book contains practical information for visitors as well as for prospective residents..."   *--Transitions Abroad*

"OUTSTANDING! [The Grays] have done a fantastic job of weaving personal interest items into a factual guide."
--Coble International

"Much more than a "retirement" guide...I felt like I had a guide by my side visiting Belize. No matter what you have heard about Belize, good or bad, put it all out of your mind as you read this first hand story by the authors that have lived in Belize...[They] have put together an excellent "picture" of Belize...you can see it, hear it, feel it and taste it! Along with this picture, they provide you with valuable contacts in Belize and the U.S.A. that can help you and save you money. Where to stay, where to eat, what to see...a complete guide book!"   *--Worldwide Investment News*

Belize Retirement Guide
The book that shows you how to live in a tropical paradise on $450 a month!

BELIZE
Retirement Guide
How to Live in a Tropical Paradise
on $450 a Month

By
Bill and Claire Gray

Fourth edition, completely revised

Preview Publishing

Belize Retirement Guide
How to Live in a Tropical Paradise on $450 a Month
By Bill & Claire Gray

Published By:
PREVIEW PUBLISHING
Post Office Box 1179
Pine Valley, CA 91962 U.S.A.

Copyright © 1990, 1993, 1995, 1996, 1999 by Bill & Claire Gray
First Printing 1990
Second Printing 1991
Third Printing 1992
Fourth Printing 1993, revised
Fifth Printing 1994
Sixth Printing 1995, completely revised
Seventh Printing 1996, revised
Eighth Printing 1999, completely revised

Library of Congress Cataloging in Publication Data

Gray, Bill, date.
Belize retirement guide: how to live in a tropical paradise on $450 a month / by Bill & Claire Gray.--4th ed., completely revised.
     p. cm.
Bibliography: p.
Includes index.
ISBN 1-880862-47-6: $29.95 Softcover
    I. Belize--Description and travel--1981-Guide-books.
    2. Retirement, Place of--Belize. 3. Caribbean living, facilities, etc.--Belize--Directories. I. Gray, Claire. I I. Title.
    917.28204'5--dc 20   CIP 91-078281

Contents

Progresso Lagoon

Chapter 1
Tropical Paradise

The first time we went to Belize in the 1980's we didn't know what to expect, only having heard it was the "ends of the earth." We were pleasantly surprised. We loved the tropical climate, the palm trees and the polite people. We loved it so much, a few months later we loaded everything we owned into a 35 foot long retired school bus and moved to Belize.

We found ourselves living in a lovely 3 bedroom house, next door to a hotel on a sun-drenched tropical bay. We could walk out our door and into the 85° sparkling clear, turquoise water that Belize is famous for. We could also eat delicious tropical fruits and fresh seafood whenever we wanted. In California, where we're from, only millionaires could afford to live like this. But we weren't millionaires, far from it. We were living on a very small amount of money. We wondered why more people weren't doing the same thing. Then we realized they didn't know they could.

We started getting letters from friends, friends of friends, and even complete strangers, all asking the same questions: "How did you do it?" "How can I do it?" We'd write letters back and answer their questions. At one point Bill suggested we write a book. I immediately snapped back with the reply: "That's the most ridiculous idea I've ever heard. Besides, the last thing in the world I want to do is write a book!"

Perhaps more than anything else the experience of Marion, our friend and neighbor in Belize, prompted us to write this book. We realized how common this story could be:

Marion had lived in Iowa all of her 63 years. But she never got used to the cold. It seemed to get worse the older she got. The wind just cut right through her. The last two years she suffered chill blains. She said that was just about the worst pain she had ever had.

Marion and her husband had farmed all their lives. After he was gone, she had only a $352 monthly Social Security check to live on. That was all; no pension, no life insurance, it was hard, but somehow she did it. Marion always said: "We never had much, never needed much."

Her apartment was small and dark, and in the summer it got very stuffy. But that wasn't nearly as bad as the winters. She couldn't seem to stay warm, no matter what she did. If it weren't for the assistance she got with heating, she would not have been able to pay the bills.

One day Marion's friend Gladys, told her about a *60 Minutes* program she had seen on TV. They showed a place called Belize. Marion had never even heard of it. Gladys said it was a small country where the people spoke English, and the cost of living was very low. She said it was warm there all the time, that's the part Marion liked!

Gladys was so excited that she wanted to go check it out right away. Marion couldn't afford to go with her, but told her she would wait for her report. Gladys went for 2 weeks and loved it. She said it was warm, the people were friendly and she loved the palm trees.

They figured that if the two of them shared a house, they could live pretty well on their combined $700 a month.

Even though she was 68, Gladys wanted to drive down. She bought a used van; within a month they loaded their things and took off.

They've never regretted their move to Belize. Everyone at home had kind of made fun of them--saying they were going to live in some hut in the jungle. But, they live in a beautiful house--nicer than any place they had lived in the U.S.

They both feel wonderful, the warmer it gets the better Marion feels. Sometimes Gladys complains that it's hot--but you should see her. Back home she suffered greatly with arthritis in her spine. But in Belize, she is much better. She doesn't know if it's the sunshine, or the warm ocean water, or both. She even began walking a couple of miles a day. And as for Marion, she enjoys walking so much, that she sold her car!

Marion went back home to visit her children last summer. She missed Belize so much, that she couldn't wait to get back!

We began to see that a book on how to retire in Belize would fill a real need. We saw people living in Belize on Social Security who would be eking out a meager existence in the U.S.

But we want to tell you up front that Belize isn't for everyone. . . and are we glad for that! Usually people either love it or hate it. I don't know why it elicits such a strong response in people, but it does, we've seen it over and over again.

Let us be the first to let you know Belize is not perfect. If you're looking for a cut-rate Hawaii, look elsewhere. Belize is not for the faint hearted with its rough and tumble style. It's called the Wild West of the Caribbean for good reason. Belize is the least developed country in Central America and one of the least developed in the world. So don't expect much in the way of amenities.

But for some of us, it's just what we're looking for. For example, Emory King an American writer was shipwrecked here in 1953 and has been in Belize ever since, he says: "I still love it."

If punctuality and organization are of foremost importance to you, don't move to Belize--you won't be happy. But if you are willing to change; to adapt to the mellowed out Belizean way of doing things, you may be in for a wonderful surprise. . .

Caye Caulker

Chapter 2
Belize? . . . What's Belize?

On a hot, August afternoon, my mother-in-law, father-in-law, some good friends and I sat on lawn chairs in a driveway in Oceanside, California. The driveway was filled with tables and the tables were filled with junk --our junk or as my mother-in-law says: "Collectors items." Junk though it was, it was a cut above the typical garage sale junk. We were preparing to move out of the country--my in-laws and I--and we were liquidating our assets. Our friend Donna had lovingly offered her driveway for the task.

As the usual cast of garage sale characters milled about, one woman stood out. She was quite large and clad in polyester, with her chestnut hair in kind of a 1964 bouffant style. "Why are ya' all selling all these nice things?" She drawled, surveying the potpourri. "These people are all moving to Belize!" Donna answered. The woman then said something that I'll never forget: "Bell-eats? . . . What's Bell-eats?"

You see, not only did she not know where Belize was--or how to pronounce it for that matter! (Belize rhymes with breeze). She didn't know what it was.

Mention Belize to most people, and you'll almost always get a blank look back. Tell them it used to be called British Honduras, and most will have a glimmer of recognition. Of course, many will then get it confused with "Spanish"

Honduras, and will start telling you about the problems it has and the American troops there.   When you tell them that you are talking about a completely different country, they may not even notice--at the most, it will seem like a minor point. We don't know why, but that invariably happens.

Then there are those who "know" all about Belize or think they do. You are bound to hear: "That's in the Mid-East right?" or "Oh yeah, Belize, know it well . . . What part of Africa is that in again? . . . I forget."

Bill will never forget the travel agent who, when asked--unhesitatingly said yes, he did have some information on Belize. Bill was pleasantly surprised, since no one else did. The man started looking in his Europe file, then said he couldn't find the information there although he was certain Belize was in Europe. Bill suggested looking under Caribbean. "No, no," the man said as he went through his South Pacific file. Somewhere in the middle of his Tahiti file, Bill mentioned Central America. No comment from the increasingly frustrated travel agent, who had now decided Belize was in the Solomon Islands.

After refusing to look under either Caribbean or Central America, the man escorted Bill to the door. He said, oh yes, he remembered now, that there were two Belizes, but that right now he was out of information on both of them!

Yes, there is some misinformation about Belize; but more often than not, there is no information circulating about Belize. And it's still exceedingly difficult to obtain good information. We know, we searched high and low for a book on Belize before we made our first trip. We finally found one; and we do mean one, literally--at that time there was only one book about Belize in print.

So now, to answer the question of our garage sale customer: "What is Bell-eats?" Belize is a country, a very tiny country, but a country nonetheless.

It is not part of another country, as some think. It is located just below Mexico, about 200 miles south of Cancun and next to Guatemala. It is the nothernmost country in Central America; (Remember that, it's a Trivial Pursuit question!) bordered on its east coast by the Caribbean.

It is considered both a Central American country and part of the Caribbean. It is very tropical, lush and green-- warm all the time. A place of great natural beauty. Most of Belize is still untouched.

The following illustrates how confused people are about Belize: A friend's family took a trip to Cancun. They rented a car and headed south. They eventually hit Belize. Apparently they entered the country and spent some time there--how long we do not know. But they never knew that they were in another country. They reported back to their friends in the States: "If you drive far enough into Mexico, you come to a place where people start speaking English again!"

Yes, Belize is bordered by Mexico and Guatemala, but it is not part of either of them. Although Guatemala has at times claimed that Belize belongs to her--it doesn't. It seems that Britain reneged on some sort of "wild" road building agreement with the Spanish a couple of hundred years ago; then Guatemala claimed Belize was their "compensation" for not getting a road cut through to the Caribbean coast.

In 1783 British ownership was recognized by the *Peace of Paris*. This was confirmed by the United States in 1850 by the *Clayton-Bulwer Treaty*. From 1862 onward it was ruled by England as a regular colony and called British Honduras. In 1871 it became an independent crown colony. It's capital was Belize, now called Belize City (and no longer the Capital). In 1961 British Honduras became self governing and in 1981, fully independent and officially called Belize. Its "new" Capital is Belmopan, population 4,000.

Belize is very much its own country. It is in Central America, yes, but it doesn't quite seem to belong there. But then, where does it belong? No one seems to know.

Different in every way, Belize has a culture, food, language, and people all its own, and Belize is fiercely proud of these differences. The moment you cross the border into Belize, you can see, taste, and smell the differences.

From the Caribbean style clapboard houses, perched precariously up on wooden stilts, to the rice cooked in coconut milk, Belize is different.

Everything we've ever read on Belize has used the same word to describe it. . . "surreal". . . and we feel inclined to use that word ourselves.

Imagine seeing a horse drawn buggy full of blue-eyed-blond white folks in bib overalls and straw hats, the women in pinafores and bonnets--right out of the 1800's. Now imagine that buggy sharing a coconut lined dirt road with an air-conditioned bus. The bus filled to the bursting point with brown skinned people grooving to the beat of Reggae--both disappear into the jungle mist. It's. . . well. . . surreal.

It's as if once you step into Belize you step back in time. It's hard for us to put our finger on exactly what it is, but we feel it, and so do many others.

One can say that Mexico is a developing country in the 20th century. But Belize seems more like rural America at the turn of the century--with a bit of a tropical, Third World twist.

Aldous Huxley said it best when he wrote: "If the world has any ends, [Belize] would certainly be one of them. It is not on the way from anywhere to anywhere."

So, why then, you ask, would anyone want to go there?

Chapter 3
Why Belize?

A myriad of reasons make Belize a delightful place to retire. We'll touch on some of them here.

Belize is an English speaking country

If you have traveled much in foreign countries where you didn't know the language, you'll recognize this as a tremendous plus. Especially when you're going to be living there, rather than vacationing for a few weeks. So many problems are eliminated. Can you imagine going to the hospital with chest pains at 3 a.m. and not being able to communicate with the doctor?

Remember, Belize used to be a British colony, so the national language became English. The schools teach in English. All the signs are in English, as well as government forms.

The local people prefer to speak Creole, an English dialect. It's similar to what is spoken in Jamaica, with a lot of "Yes mon's." They call what we North American's speak "High English," and can speak it if they want to.

You won't be able to understand their Creole at first, without straining. But just tell them: "I'm sorry, I don't understand the Creole yet." They will be most obliging. Unfortunately even after they switch to regular English, it may be difficult to understand because of their accent. But you'll catch on very quickly.

What is unique about Belize is that you can learn a foreign language if you want to, but you don't have to. You see, virtually all Belizeans are bilingual (actually many are trilingual). Spanish and English are used interchangeably. Radio and television commercials are done first in English, then Spanish. It's great if you're trying to learn Spanish.

Maya is a very soft sounding language and is spoken in many parts of the country--especially the southern half. The Indians remain quite isolated in their remote villages, so you won't hear Maya spoken as much as Spanish.

Low German or "Plattdeutsch" as they call it, is spoken by the Mennonites. (More about them later). We have a friend who learned furniture making from the Mennonites and ended up speaking fluent German.

And whether you want to or not, if you stay long enough, you'll learn Creole. Whether you choose to speak it or not is another matter entirely. Some Gringos do-- some don't--it's up to you.

Belize is a great place to relax

In Belize things are laid back--way back. No one is in a hurry to do anything --ever. That includes the clerk waiting on you in the store and the postal service delivering your mail.

That makes some people frustrated and very nervous. But many retirees find that the slow pace in Belize is just their speed. They, possibly for the first time in their lives, completely unwind, and enjoy life. Isn't that what retirement is all about?

Belize is a healthy place to live

Industry is almost nonexistent in Belize; so few people live there, and have so few cars, that the air is unbelievably clean. Belize is about as pollution free as any place can be in this day and age.

The lifestyle in Belize is healthy; fresh food; fresh air;

lots of sunshine, lots of walking, and no stress.   Sounds like a prescription from the doctor, doesn't it?

Belize is an inexpensive place to live

Belize has one of the lowest costs of living in the world. This may seem hard to believe, when you see a box of breakfast cereal selling for $7. In fact, Belize can be very expensive, especially for vacationers with a reckless attitude toward finances; and for us Americans, who may insist on having exactly what we are used to at home. Take the breakfast cereal for example, in the States it's an inexpensive breakfast.   But in Belize, it's an imported food item and exorbitantly priced.   On the other hand, sweet juicy mangoes are a real delicacy in the U.S. and sell for up to $2 each; but in Belize they can sell for about 15 cents. So, with some adapting on your part, you can eat meals that are both delicious and inexpensive.

It's generally said that Belize is the most expensive place in Central America but the least expensive in the Caribbean. Prices in Belize are very stable. Recently, the annual rate of inflation has been around 2.8%. If anything it seems that prices are staying the same or even going down. Maybe it's because Belize is becoming less isolated than it once was, the roads are better, and now it's easier to get to.

When we say you can live in Belize on $450 a month we don't mean that everything in Belize is cheap. What we do mean is that you can enjoy a higher standard of living on that small amount of money than you can in North America.

We know many Gringos (singles and couples) who live here on $450 per person per month. Rural Peace Corps workers get a mere $350 per month for all their living expenses. And the average Belizean earns only $2,400 a year. Now, in no way are we suggesting that you could ever live as cheaply, or in the style of the average Belizean. But, they do it, and we ourselves have lived on a lot less than $450 a month. Of course, you can spend more.

Belize is politically stable

Yes, it's true. Despite all you hear about the political

problems in Central America, Belize remains untouched. Think of Belize as kind of a Central American Switzerland, politically speaking.

Frankly, no one really cares enough about Belize to invade her. Guatemala talked about it once, but never did anything. Then in 1991 the government of Guatemala for the first time recognized Belize as a sovereign nation.

Saying that their presence was "unwarranted" --British troops in 1994 officially turned over the security of Belize to the BDF (Belize Defense Force) and for the most part left Belize; leaving behind only a 500 man jungle training company.

Belize has a Parliamentary form of government with a Prime Minister and 2 political parties; the P.U.P. (Peoples United Party) and the U.D.P. (United Democratic Party). Are there any big ideological differences in the two? About the only dissimilarities we see is in their names. Each party spends most of its time and energy in office trying to undo what the other party did.

As for a coup being staged or the government being overthrown? If you'd ever been to Belize you would laugh at the very thought. No one has the motivation. Belizeans are too mellow for anything like that. Why go to all that trouble? --when you can lay in a hammock, feel the tropical breeze; and drink the sweet water of a young coconut, whenever you want to.

Belize has great weather

The average year round temperature in Belize is a balmy 79 degrees. **There is no winter; no snow, and no heating bills.** The ocean water is around 85 degrees all the time. And because the reef makes the sea water calm and shallow, it's like stepping into an enormous bathtub.

On the other hand, there is no need to cool your home with air-conditioning either, the breeze coming off the Caribbean will do that for you. The most you need to keep you cool is a fan. We've never been in a Belizean home that had air-conditioning. Some say the climate in Belize is milder than Florida; cooler in the summer and warmer in the winter.

Belize isn't that far away

Not far away for a foreign country that is --it's not as far as Argentina, or Guam. From Brownsville Texas, going south down the East Coast of Mexico it's 1,350 road-miles to Belize. You can drive it in a few days. There are daily flights in and out of Belize. So it's possible to travel back and forth quickly. You can fly from Belize to Miami in an hour and a half.

Belize has an excellent phone system compliments of the Queen. England gave them a state of the art fiber optic phone system. A sort of going away present after receiving independence.

You can call Belize from anywhere in the U.S. and vice versa. From the U.S. to Belize economy rates bring the cost down to 30 cents per minute. From Belize to the U.S. the rate is: $1.60 per minute 4 a.m. to 11 p.m. (Belize time). From 10 p.m. to 6 a.m. the rate is $1 per minute.

Belize has an excellent postal service, based on the English postal system. There are daily mail shipments from Belize to Miami and vice versa. You can usually expect to get mail from the U.S. about a week to a week and a half after it's mailed to Belize. This is phenomenal considering the region. I mailed a letter to Mexico City from Belize, and it took no less than 6 months. Friends in Guatemala say, mailing something from there, is like dropping it into an inter-galactic black hole.

As a foreigner in Belize you can:
Live as a resident

Belize offers Permanent Residency status to foreigners from almost any country. The cost is $300 for an individual or family head and $50 each for spouse or children. You can live in Belize full or part time without giving up your present citizenship. With Belizean Permanent Residency you have all the rights of a Belizean citizen except, the right to vote or serve in the military.

We aren't saying there isn't any red tape involved, but compared to other countries it's relatively easy, quick and inexpensive. (For more details as well as all necessary government forms, see our Special Report: *How to Become a Resident of Belize*).

As a foreigner in Belize you can:
Own Land

That's right, unlike Mexico, as a foreigner you can buy land in Belize and own it outright with fully marketable title. It's yours to do whatever you want to with it. It's in your name; you can leave it to your children in your will, and there is no inheritance tax in Belize. And also, the government of Belize will give you land practically free! Once you receive your residency, you can apply for a piece of land from the government (for more detailed information and government forms see our Special Report: *Buying Property/Building a House in Belize*).

As a foreigner in Belize you can:
Work or start a business

Foreigners can work and earn money in Belize (unlike so many other countries) but you must have either a work permit or Permanent Residency. Foreigners can even start businesses. (For more information see our Special Report: *Starting a Business / Working in Belize*)

You'll find there are very few restrictions on what you can do and how you can do it. For example, Belizeans fix up the spare bedroom and hang out a "Hotel" sign and they're in the hotel business. They put out a table and chairs; cook up a batch of cheeseburgers, serve them on the front porch and they're a restaurateur It's that simple, at least for Belizeans. Someone once said you can be anything you want in Belize. It's true. There's a sense of freedom in Belize not found many places, especially not in the U.S., where red tape can tie you up for years. I guess that's why some have called Belize an entrepreneurs paradise.

There's lots to see and do in Belize

You'll be taken by the unspoiled scenery and endless variety of fauna and flora found in this small country. Undiscovered archaeological sites spatter the virgin rain-forest. Majestic waterfalls paint the mountains and gorges with crystal clear water. And the sunny cayes have some of the best sportsfishing, scuba, and skin diving in the Western Hemisphere. . . But then you'll have to see all this for yourself.

Fishing boat near Copper Bank

Chapter 4
Getting to Belize

Driving to Belize is a real trip (yes, the pun was intended). Depending on your attitude, the trip can either be the worst experience of your life or one of the most interesting and delightful. We consider it the latter, and so do many other North Americans we know, who have made the trek. And we do know several, including one American friend who has lived in Belize for 20 years, and has made the trip 49 times!

As previously mentioned, the route used most often to get to Belize is through Southern Texas. At either Brownsville or McAllen, cross the border into Mexico. The McAllen route is about 50 miles shorter, if you are coming from the western half of the United States. Then just hug the East Coast of Mexico all the way down south; going through Tampico, Veracruz, and Villahermosa. I know some who have done this stretch of road in as little as 2 days!

Of course you can drive to Belize a number of other ways: Including down the West Coast of Mexico, or through Baja California when the ferry is running from La Paz to Mazatlan. But we have noticed that people who regularly drive to Belize, never go that way. They stay in the U.S., as long as possible, and then crossover in Southern Texas.

However, there are 18 entry points on the U.S./Mexico border, and you could use any of these to get to Belize.

To enter Mexico you need only a Tourist Card. You can get one at the border, free of charge. You can also obtain a Transit Visa, through the Mexican consulate nearest you if you want. But we've found it's best to be considered a tourist in Mexico. So plan some sightseeing, and don't even mention you're headed for Belize until you get to Chetumal (the last town in Mexico before you get to Belize). Getting a Transit Visa might open a real can of worms, costing you time and money.

For information: Call (800) 446-3942 Mexico Tourism Information Service), Or the Fax Me Mexico service at (541) 385-9282. Website: //http:mexico-travel.com/. Or write to: 21 East 63rd St., 3rd fl., New York, NY 10021.

At the Mexican border they will issue you a vehicle permit. If you just bought a car for the trip and the title is not in your name yet, you can ask your local Department of Motor Vehicles for a "Mexican Letter" explaining this fact, as registration alone, usually won't do it.

The Mexicans insist that the driver be the same person who's name is on the title and registration. The driver must get the permit to import the vehicle. After clearing Immigration; show *Banjercito* (pronounced: BON HAIR SEE TOE) your title, registration, drivers license, and credit card. They will fill out the importation forms for you. **Make sure you get copies of all paper work** (they have Xerox machines). Next, pay the cashier a $12 fee. This fee must be paid with a major credit card (Visa, MasterCard or American Express). The only agency that can legally issue this holographic sticker is *Banjercito*. Look for the name, and don't buy it from anyone else, or you're buying a fake. Next a Customs official checks all your papers for accuracy, signs your permit, and stamps your passport "Con Vehiculo" (with vehicle) while a Banjercito employee puts a pretty holographic sticker on your windshield.

The Mexican government has had a lot of trouble with American cars entering, but not leaving Mexico (especially Chevys). Taxi drivers have a liking for American Chevrolets. They may even offer to buy yours from you, then swap papers with a wreck . . . and presto, a "Mexican" taxi is born.

About a half hour south of the border you'll run into a checkpoint, don't worry, this is merely to see if you have the required paper-work.

The Mexican government wants a guarantee that your car will leave with you, and if it doesn't they want you to pay the duty. We think we understand why they feel this way. Years before they had the Banjercito credit card arrangement, we "involuntarily" left our car in Tampico. About a year later, we received a surprise letter and check from a Mexican family, telling us that they had fixed our car, sold it, and wanted us to have half the money! We were moved by the honesty of our new found friends, but mystified as to how they were ever able to repair our pile of twisted metal.

When you leave Mexico, tell Banjercito that you're taking your car with you, and they'll remove the sticker from your windshield and take your name out of the computer. Save the receipt in case there's a problem.

How long will it take you to drive to Belize? No one ever knows. There are just too many variables, one being your personal pace. You can head out of Matamoros like Mario Andretti on Vivarin, stopping only long enough to refuel your car and body, or you can savor the charm of each village you pass through, stopping to sample the ambiance along with the local tamales. The other major variable will be the road/weather conditions. These two are closely connected because basically, when it rains a lot the roads are horrible. The problems you might encounter range from potholes--some tremendous in size--to bridges being washed out completely.

Some roads in Mexico are quite good, especially in the dry season, December through June. The roads as a general rule, tend to worsen as you go farther south. Really, they aren't bad at all until you get into Yucatan. If you've planned your trip for October (the height of the rainy season), don't despair, you can still do it. We have.

Always follow the cardinal rule of driving in Mexico: **DON'T DRIVE AT NIGHT!** There are a number of reasons why--all of them serious and potentially dangerous: Many Mexicans think it is safer to drive with their lights off. They say the lights cause glare. This could be true, but what happens when you meet one of these guys on a dark stormy night, taking a blind curve a little too fast? There are so many hazards to look for in your average Mexican road anyway--everything from the aforementioned pot holes, to cows. The last thing you need is a veil of darkness to make things even more difficult.

It's said, that because the road retains the heat from the sun, animals actually seek out the warm asphalt at night as a place to lie down. Sounds quaint, doesn't it? At least until you total the front end of your $30,000 Land Rover on a Brahman bull.

Always get Mexican car insurance before you cross the border. You can get Mexican insurance in the U.S., through AAA, if you're a member, and could do so before you start your trip. Or you can wait and get it on the U.S. side of any border crossing. Expect to pay about $5 a day.

Sanborns is a good company that offers a lot of services, including a *Travelog*, a handy little book that takes you mile by mile down the road, through Mexico and into Belize. There is also the "Trip Share Service" for those who don't want to go it alone.

You can write to them and request a *Mexico Travel-Aid & Trip-Planner* at: Sanborn Insurance, 2011 South 10th St.,

McAllen, Texas 78503. Or call (800) 222-0158 for quotes and insurance by mail or fax. For a *Travelog* and questions about Mexico, call: (800) 638-9423.

Please remember: **All non-Mexican insurance is invalid in Mexico,** and you don't want to be involved in an accident in Mexico without it. If you are, you can be held in jail until all claims are settled or you can prove your ability to pay --and no one can help you, not even the American Embassy. Embassy personnel do not interfere with matters involving Mexican law.

Here's a tip: When you purchase your Mexican insurance you'll receive a sticker to put in the window of your car, showing that you are insured by such and such company. This is not required, it's just free advertising. Don't put the insurance sticker in your window! You could be intentionally hit so the other party can collect insurance money.

What should you do if you are involved in an accident? Try and get away before the police arrive. Shocked? We know that might be hard to swallow and it goes against our North American sensibilities but, in Mexico it's not against the law to leave the scene of an accident.

Even if you are insured, do not stop if you are involved in a minor accident, just keep on going. If it's not so minor and you feel that you damaged the other guy's car, stop. . . apologize, give him some cash and take off before the police arrive. If he's injured, you can take him in your car to the nearest hospital or doctors office.

That's the way it's done in Mexico. You handle it yourself; you can leave the scene of the accident as quickly as possible, drive yourself to the nearest hospital or doctor and have yourself checked out for whiplash, possible heart attack and anything else you can think of. Then contact your insurance company and notify the police--in that order. That advice comes from a friend we have in the

Federales (Mexican Highway Patrol).
If you should see a terrible accident.   It's best not to stop, because when the Police arrive you may end up paying for someone else's accident. You will want to avoid contact with the Mexican Police at the scene of an accident where you will be most vulnerable.

Once, while towing an old Volkswagen van down to Belize, we were involved in an accident just outside a sleepy little village called Chuatemoc, perched on the side of a hill.

As we traveled up the winding road through this village, children lined the streets. There was a huge and unusual looking oversized truck coming slowly toward us, carrying a colossal hydroelectric generator on its bed. Men were standing on top of the generator with forked sticks and dead tree limbs propping up the power lines as they drove under them. We stopped to let them pass.

The spectacle of this huge truck lumbering through the village, plus some crazy Gringo RV'ers pulling a van was the entertainment for the villagers that quiet Sunday morning.

The truck passed.   No sooner had we started up again when we heard: POW! POW! POW! A loud metallic sound comes from somewhere. Bill checks the mirrors: "It's not us." Then CRASH! "Some jerk must have had an accident" Bill says. Then followed the most peculiar sound of metal and chain scraping the road. I stick my head out the window to see our van, crashed off on the side of the road! Suddenly, I realized there are children all around it, all of them with their eyes big as saucers. I had to look to see if any children were under the van. . . None, OK, whew!

Apparently the bolts in our tow bar had broken, the van disconnected from us and then wrapped itself around a cement abutment on a culvert. Fortunately, there was no damage to anyone or anything except to our van. If it had been a few feet to the right or to the left it could have gone into someone's living room. Or worse, right below where it stopped was a house with a big front yard and a store on the front porch.

The yard was filled with people, watching the "show" on the road. If that cement thing hadn't been there the van would have just kept going and plowed into the yard full of people. Not to mention the group of children it had gone through without hitting one of them. It was as if a giant hand had placed our van in the exact spot where it would cause the least amount of damage to people or property.

Suddenly there were people everywhere. (How does everyone find out everything so fast in these villages where there are no telephones?) In about two minutes, a little old beat up Toyota Taxi screeches to a halt. Out of the passenger side steps the town constable. He looked like he was right out of central casting; with his big black mustache, rumpled uniform buttoned over an ample belly, and 2-days growth of beard. Slightly hung over, he swaggered up and began to survey the situation.

A minute or so later a blue pickup truck packed with police pulls up. They ranged in age from about 16 to 80 and everyone had a rifle over his shoulder. All 12 of them climb out of the back and swarm the scene. We got a little nervous, remembering stories we had heard about the Mexican Police. They too, examine the accident.

A long tense minute or so goes by and then they say to each other--right in front of our traveling companion Ruby, never dreaming she can understand Spanish: "Aw! This isn't worth trying to get any money out of. . . Let's go!" They all jump back onto their truck and speed off down the road as quickly as they had come.

We were relieved to say the least.

In this part of the world, the police are always looking

for a quick buck. Remember this if you get in an accident.

Getting Gas

We've got this down to a science. You can get cheated badly in Mexican gas stations. You can also take charge of the situation and never get cheated at all.

Here's what to do: Get a locking gas cap. Then make some kind of a label stating the capacity of your gas tank. For example: "Capacidad 80 litros" (Capacity 80 liters--or 20 gallons). Stick it on your car next to the gas cap. This will prove invaluable when you are presented with a bill for 87 liters of gas.

Sometimes attendants try to distract you, so that it's difficult to check the pump before they start (make sure it starts at zero). Watch out for filling stations where a mob of kids run up and start washing all your windows at the same time, and be especially careful of the stations where all the attendants are females--wearing skimpy hot pants. Unless you have that locking cap, they'll start putting gas in, even before your car has stopped moving.

Don't let them do this. You control the situation. You get out with the key. You unlock it. You stand there with calculator in hand, watching every number that whizzes by; look serious, look imposing.

When the pump stops, note your total immediately, it may only be there a few seconds before they go on to another customer. Have them show you on your calculator, the number of liters you bought, times the number of pesos per liter. The total may look scary....Say, you're figuring 80 liters of gas times 4.5 pesos per liter...it equals 360 pesos! Sounds expensive, until you figure it out at 20 gallons of gas for $36.

See why you need a calculator? Make them show it to you on your calculator, at least twice. Scrutinize everything

--the number of liters, and the price.

Make it seem hard to cheat you. If they are trying to, they will give up at some point--if you stand firm. Refuse to pay until they prove they are right. Even if I think I've gotten all of my change back, I still keep my hand outstretched as if to receive more. You'd be surprised at how often the operator will sheepishly cough up more money after he has already stopped counting.

Where should you buy gas? Pemex, the government run oil company is your only choice. One thing you don't have to worry about in Mexico is finding the best price. The fuel prices are controlled by the government, so all gas stations from one end of the country to the other have the same prices.

What kind of gas should you use? Magna Sin (pronounced MAGNA-SEEN) is very good. But, just recently, Mexico introduced Premium (pronounced PRAY-ME-OOM) and we recommend it highly. It's a bit more expensive than Magna Sin, but well worth it, if you need the higher octane. Both of these are very good super-unleaded fuels. In fact, we make regular trips across the border to buy Magna Sin, because we like the price and quality better than the American made gas that's sold in Belize.

Pemex finally got rid of its infamous Nova gasoline! It was a cheap gas, that used to leave your car dancing the bossa nova minutes after you had shut off the engine. "Dieseling" like that, was bad on the rings, and use to damage a lot of engines. I learned to do like the Mexicans, and put my car in gear before turning it off. So, I'm glad it's gone. Good-riddance!

Whenever we need gas in Mexico, we stop and ask: "Hay Magna Sin?" (pronounced "EYE MAGNA SEEN?") "Is there Magna Sin?" Any time you see a green triangle-shaped sign along the highway, it means a Pemex station is coming up.

You won't see gas stations as frequently in Mexico as you do in the U.S., and they will usually be located at the edge of towns and at major crossroads.

Breaking Down

Tell a friend in the U.S. that you're planning a long drive through Mexico and down to Belize and they no doubt will say: "But what if you break down?" Everyone seems obsessed with this idea of a Gringo being stranded somewhere out there in the vast Mexican desert--mustachioed bandidos crawling out of every crevice. Well, without hesitation we can say that we feel we are more safe, and more assured of getting help quicker in Mexico than in many parts of the U.S.

We say as a general rule you're better off in Mexico. Why? Because by nature the people are more caring, more concerned, more helpful and also great "mechanics." We've seen them--from small boys to old men--crawl inside the engine compartment, at a moments notice and start-in.

While we are still reading the car manual, they start improvising tools and parts. That piece of pipe in the trunk can take on new value, etc.

For example, we had a friend who destroyed his drive shaft going over a piece of rough road. A couple of these amateur "mechanics" took a piece of metal sewer pipe and two U-joints, and after some artful welding, our friend had a new drive shaft; that he claims was still working last time I talked to him. You may cringe at their methods, but they will get you there.

The Mexican government sponsors teams of roving mechanics called the "Green Angels." Their sole purpose is to comb the highways and find people having car trouble and to help them. These uniformed, English speaking officers patrol during all daylight hours. Minor repairs and adjustments are free. You pay for any parts or materials needed. . . What more could a tourist ask for?

Once years ago, my car caught fire on a busy street in Los Angeles. I hadn't realized what was happening and flames quickly engulfed my small car. I narrowly escaped. A crowd gathered to watch my car burn, and as I stood on the sidewalk shaking, a Los Angeles policeman screamed at me: "You better move that car lady! It's blocking traffic!" Yes, I'd say you're better off in Mexico.

By Train

Mexico has an extensive train system that we are dying to try. Although there is no train that goes all the way to Belize, you can get to Merida, in Yucatan. From there, you can connect with a bus that takes you to Chetumal, the very last Mexican city that borders Belize. To get to Merida by train however, you have to take a 27 hour ride from Mexico City, on a second class train--the cost is about $10.

The train is less expensive than the bus. A first class train ticket costs about three-quarters of the price of a first class bus ride. Second class is even cheaper, but usually not acceptable by tourist standards.

However, since Mexico began revamping their trains a few years ago second class is not as bad as it used to be. Sometimes, it's better to request "Primera Especial" (Special 1st Class) when available. You may also be able to get sleeping accommodations. Although some say the reclining seats in first class are so comfortable they have no trouble sleeping in them.

For detailed information on riding the rails anywhere in Mexico we strongly suggest you get a copy of: *Mexico By Rail* by Gary Poole. It's published by a slightly reclusive British company called Hunter Publishing, with a U.S. address in Edison, New Jersey of all places! (See Resources)

You can write and request information on schedules and fares in English or even make your reservations by mail, one or two months in advance. For more information as well as reservations on Mexican Railroads write to: Señor Larraquival, Chief Commercial Passenger Dept., National Railways Mexico, Buenavista Grand Central Station, 06358 Mexico, D.F., Tel. 547-86-55 or 800-321-1699 (Mexico by Train).

By Boat

Mile after mile of lush reefs. . . sparkling white atolls and uninhabited cayes. . . sailing to Belize and the Western Caribbean might just be the adventure you're looking for.

If you're fortunate enough to get to Belize under sail you'll find that not much is required--no boat visa, cruising permit, tourist cards, or complicated stuff like that.   All you need is your passport, vessel documentation and clearance from your last port of call--the usual.

Have ready: Four copies of your crew and passenger manifests; four copies of your stores and cargo lists (ballast in cargo).   There is no entry fee.   All vessels are required to clear customs and immigration.

When buying charts for Belize, get the British charts-- they're more detailed than the newer American ones.   Be aware that the reef has grown 6 feet or more in some places and not everything will be exactly where the older charts (Circa 1830) show it to be, but these are still the best charts to use.

When coming from the north via Mexico, your port of entry will "usually" be Belize City (more about this later).

Enter Belize City flying a yellow quarantine flag and tie up alongside the Radisson Fort George dock. Their radio frequency is 68. They have a base station on the dock and in the hotel--with the dockmaster carrying a mobile unit-- use channel 16 if necessary.   It's 60¢ per foot per night, plus 15% VAT.   Tel. 501-2-33333 or 1-800-333-3333.

The Captain is allowed to go ashore to notify customs (Tel. 02-77092, Fax: 02-77015). The dockmaster will call them for you and also notify immigration and the health department at the same time. A boarding party will meet you at your boat. Although Belize has no entry fee, you will be required to reimburse the customs, immigration, and health officers for their taxi fare. This will cost around $10. Also it's kind of an unwritten "practice" or you might even call it a "tradition" to have cold beers ready for the officials when they arrive on board. If you forget, they may remind you.

Give them the beers first, then your paper work, in that order--but don't open the beers just yet, they may decide they want them "to go." They'll stamp a 30 day visitors permit into your passport. For an extension, take a cab to Belize City Immigration at Mahogany St. Extension.

A lot of nations don't have a love affair with guns like we Americans do. If you have any weapons on board. . . declare them now! They'll allow you to keep a shotgun, but will impound all other firearms. They'll place them in bonded storage and return them cleaned and oiled if you check out. (This only applies to boats. Don't try to bring in firearms by land or air!) If you do not declare them, and they're found. . . you're in trouble! Take a walk down by the Belize City jail and you'll see what kind of trouble I mean.

It's now possible to check-in at 2 other courtesy ports: San Pedro, Ambergris Caye--every other Wednesday at 9:00 a.m.--from the Town Board Hall; and daily, in the south from the Punta Gorda Police Station.

If you're just "gunk-holeing" and eventually plan to move on when the mood strikes you, here's how you check out: from Belize City.

(1) Take all your papers to customs on Caesar Ridge Road.
(2) Then on to Port Authority, next door at King's Pier;

Pay a clearance fee of $10 plus a 75¢ per ton   "Aids to Navigation Fee." Take the clearance paper and receipt they give you back to customs. (3) Customs will then give you bilingual "zarpe" forms (in Spanish and English) for your next port of call. (4) Your last stop is immigration, leave them a copy of your crew and passenger manifest. *Note: If you check-in and out through either of the courtesy ports (San Pedro or PG) you won't be charged a clearance fee.*

To sail through Mexican waters from Belize, get a *Tourist Card* and a *Temporary Boat Visa* from the Mexican Consulate at: 20 N. Park St. on the corner of Marine Parade and Park St. in Belize City. Tel. 02-30194/Fax: 02-78742.

By Bus

The subject of riding buses in Mexico and Belize deserves a book of its own. In Mexico alone, the system is so large, that there are over 700 bus lines --Belize is a different story, though. So no matter where you're starting from you can certainly get to Belize by bus. One rule of thumb: **Always go first class** (in Mexico it's "Primera clase"). Belizean buses are usually all one class. The closest you can get to a "First Class" bus in Belize is an Express bus.

You can buy your tickets for destination's in Mexico through Greyhound/Trailways in the U.S. Be sure to remember, that to get to Belize, you first have to go to the city of Chetumal, in the Mexican state of Quintana Roo. So that's the destination you'll be booking to.

From Chetumal you will be taking a Belizean bus, either Batty's or Venus, for the short hop over the border to Belize. They leave hourly: 4 a.m., to 6:30 p.m. from the *Mercado Nuevo,* (New Market). You may need to take a $1 taxi ride from one of the terminals to the market. You'll see all the Belizean buses in the New Market parking lot, you can't miss them.

Only Batty's Express buses leave from the modern Chetumal Bus Terminal. "Express" means they do not stop in the villages you will pass through, only the towns, which are Corozal, and Orange Walk.   This will cut down significantly on your travel time.

Your bus ticket between Mexico and Belize will include the border crossing. This is good. The driver will make sure your luggage gets through customs quickly (since he can't leave until it does).

When, and if you return to the U.S., you can also book your ticket through to the first town north of the border. But a word of caution: If you are going to continue your journey by bus in the U.S., wait and buy that ticket on the U.S. side.   Often there are great travel specials being offered, but only in the U.S. A Mexican or Belizean travel agent will not know about it.

By Air
There are daily flights to Belize City from New Orleans, Miami, and Houston.   The airlines that currently fly to Belize are: Taca, Continental, and American.

Always check for yourself, there could be new additions at any time. Always be sure to find out what stops are on the way. Some of these are pretty wild routes, and will have you stopping in Tegucigalpa and/or San Salvador, with the added insult of having to pay a $25 departure tax in each of the two countries that you've made unwanted stops in!

Since there aren't exactly hordes of people flocking to see Belize, airlines rarely have special fares to Belize.   But, occasionally we'll see a terrific deal on a charter flight during the winter/holiday months.

But there is a way you can fly out of the U.S., get to Belize the same day and pay only about half the plane fare to Belize city. How? There are always specials to Cancun or Cozumel, Mexico. Once you're there, that puts you just a few hours away from Belize by road. You can ride the bus the rest of the way for about $15.

Ask for "Air only," most of the these deals are a package
with a hotel stay included. But still, you may pay a lower
price than for a direct flight to Belize. You could certainly
enjoy a few days in Cancun, which by the way, if you
haven't been there, is absolutely fabulous. Before you book
your flight to Cancun, be sure to call several airlines. Try
Aero-Mexico, Mexicana, Continental, or Northwest, to
name a few. Keep checking the Sunday travel section of
your newspaper. You're bound to find a good deal to
Cancun or Cozumel.

Via Cozumel

Cozumel is an island about 20 minutes (by boat) off the
coast of Mexico and about 40 miles south of Cancun. It is
a mega-resort, developed for tourism, like Cancun. If you
want to (or have to) spend the night, there are good deals
to be found. . . even in pricey Cozumel. Just ask your taxi
driver for: "Un hotel economico." This is a sure fire way
to find a good deal on a hotel room anywhere in Mexico,
but particularly in touristy areas like Cozumel. You may
even tell your taxi driver how much you want to pay for a
room. When he takes you to a place, be sure to check-out
the room with the taxi driver present. If the room isn't to
your liking tell him so, get back in the taxi and hold out for
a better room. Even though this sounds terribly picky to
us Americans, it's perfectly acceptable to Mexicans. They
will go out of their way to please a visitor coming to their
country and won't think any less of you.

Via Playa del Carmen

We would suggest staying in Playa del Carmen rather
than Cozumel. It is more relaxed, less developed, less
expensive, and has a beach you have to see to believe. The
ocean is such a brilliant turquoise, and the sand is so
powdery white, it looks like something man-made, a movie
set of the perfect tropical beach. You can take the ferry
from Cozumel to Playa for about $5. Even though it takes
only 20 minutes, it can be a rough ride. Be prepared with

your favorite sea sickness remedy. Once in Playa del Carmen, you can either rent a car or catch a bus to Belize.

You can stay in Playa as cheaply as $3 a night--that's for a hammock on the beach. But there are other, more substantial accommodations that can be had, and inexpensively too. One great example is "El Elefante." It's rooms are large and spotlessly clean with private baths. A great bargain at $15 a night. "Lily's" is convenient, clean, safe, and right across the street from the bus station. But, the bus noise and fumes can get annoying. We're only mentioning it because it's good in a pinch; like the time we had tons of luggage to carry and didn't want to be too far from the bus station.

You can eat in Playa del Carmen inexpensively; the streets are lined with small restaurants, advertising daily specials, like half a chicken, roasted over an open fire, and served with rice, tortillas and salsa for about $3. One of our favorites is "Pollo Caribe." We wish we were there right now!

Warning! Once you see that beach at Playa del Carmen, with its white powdery sand, that "artificial" looking turquoise water, you won't ever want to leave. The first time I saw Playa del Carmen out the window of a bus, I thought it was fake. I couldn't imagine a beach looking that fantastic.

When you've had your fill of Playa, proceed to the bus station in the middle of town, near the dock; buy a ticket for the next bus to Chetumal, preferably first class. The ride from here to Belize is a little over 4 hours. Try to leave early in the day, if you want to make it over the border before the last bus to Belize leaves Chetumal at 6:30 p.m.

Via Cancun.
What to do when you arrive at the airport: Change some

of your American money or travelers checks here. They give a good rate of exchange at the airport, as does all of Cancun. This will save you from having to track down a *casa de cambio* (money exchange store).

You'll need Mexican money for incidentals on the way to Belize and possibly a hotel room. To get from the airport into town you can either take a *collectivo* or a private taxi. The *collectivo* is a little thing that looks an awful lot like a Volkswagen mini bus. . . because that's exactly what it is.

You can take a collective **from** the airport, but not **to** the airport. That's right; it's all because of a deal that was struck between the collectivo and taxi drivers. The collectivo is $2 per person. The taxi is $8 per group, so if you have a group of at least four, a taxi would cost the same and get you there faster. At this point you can head for either a place to stay the night or the bus station depending on what time your plane touches down. It can be an hour from the airport to the bus station because of traffic. And it's 5 hours more from there to Chetumal, where the last bus for Belize leaves at 6:30 p.m. Even though you could spend the night in Chetumal and cross the border in the morning, I'm sure that you would prefer spending the night in Cancun, or Playa del Carmen. We know we would. It's a nice trip through the jungle and by daylight you can see the ruins along the road.

Everyone says Cancun is expensive, but it doesn't have to be. Remember to use our tip on finding a nice, inexpensive place to stay: Just ask your taxi or collectivo driver for "un hotel economico." There are so many "Mom & Pop" inns just starting out with no money to advertise, you'll have your pick.

The last time we tried this in Cancun, we were treated to a lovely room with two large beds. It was above a restaurant, in a prime location near the bullring. The price was only $25 a night. We could have stayed somewhere else for even less money by simply telling our driver: "We want a *cuarto* (room) for $15." Try it. It sure beats carrying around a pile of budget travel guide-books; and driving all over town tracking down inexpensive hotels that are so popular now (because they're listed in that guide-book) you can't afford to stay in them.

The bus station in Cancun is small and slightly disorganized. There is no sign out front identifying it. If you're lost, ask anyone where the "terminal" (TER-ME-NALL) is.

Be sure to get a "Primera classe" (first class) ticket to Chetumal. Try to get on the express bus. There is a luxury bus that goes from Cancun to Chetumal and vice-versa. It's called "Caribe Express." The price one way, is around $20 which is roughly about $5 more than the the regular first class bus. Caribe Express offers a beautiful, new, air-conditioned bus, with lovely plush carpeting and comfortable seats. There is a rest room on board, as well as full wet bar and movie screen.

The regular First Class is "almost" hourly. Caribe Express has their own ticket window and air-conditioned waiting room at the bus station, and departs for Chetumal twice a day.

Warning! The taxi drivers that hang out at the bus station in Cancun will make all kinds of outrageous offers. Don't be a gullible Gringo. Some friends from Canada came to visit us, via Cancun. By the time they got to Belize they were irate; complaining it was "our fault" they got ripped-off for $150 by a Mexican taxi driver. We couldn't help but burst out laughing, when we found out they'd taken a taxi from Cancun to Belize (a five hour drive!).
"Why didn't you take the $15 bus?" we asked.
"Oh no." they said, "It would be $130 for the bus!"
"What! . . . Who told you that?"
"The taxi driver."
I started laughing so hard I fell down! Here's what happened: While they were standing in line for the bus to

Chetumal, a taxi driver came up and "warned" them that the bus fares had just gone up. It would cost them $130. Why not pay him $20 more and ride in his nice comfortable taxi, and they could leave right away, he said. He was so helpful, he even dropped them right at our door step.

If you should find yourself arriving in Chetumal after 6:30 p.m. when the last bus for Belize has already left. . . don't fret. You can take a taxi from Chetumal and on across the Belize border for around $10. Some Mexican taxis can take you only as far as the Mexican side of the border. You would then have to walk over the bridge to the Belize side (about a 5 minute walk). Then on the Belize side, you'd have to call a taxi. Warning: They may want to charge you up to $12.50 ($25 BZ) for the short 7 mile ride into Corozal Town. Better to find a taxi in Chetumal who can take you all the way into Corozal.

Private Plane

We're not pilots; and some of you wrote for information we didn't have, so I called the airport and this is what they told me: If you're flying yourself down to Belize, you must enter through the Phillip Goldson International Airport in Ladyville, about 10 miles outside Belize City.

The runway is 7500 feet long, 180 feet wide and fairly new, as is the terminal. The landing fees are $5 for a 6,000 lbs. aircraft, then approximately $1 for each additional 1,000 pounds.

Airspace is open during daylight hours only; 6 a.m. to 6 p.m. You're required to file a flight plan with A.F.T.N., and send a request message before entering Belizean air space. No other advance notice is required, unless you're coming from Guatemala, or Cuba. In that case; you're required to notify the Chief Aviation Officer at least 48 hours in advance. For more information call: 501-25-2014 or 2045 or 2153.

When flying down Mexico's Caribbean coast to Belize; aviation fuel is available in: Veracruz, Merida, Cancun, and Chetumal. In Belize it's available at: Phillip Goldson, Belize City Municipal Airport, and San Pedro, Ambergris Caye. Expect to pay about $4 a gallon.

All main towns and some offshore islands and Cayes have licensed airfields. None of these have hangers. Most of the runways are short, bumpy, and hard to find; but they're considered excellent for this part of the world.

For Belize weather information call the National Meteorological Service in Ladyville at 501-25-2480 or 2012.

Where in the world is Belize?

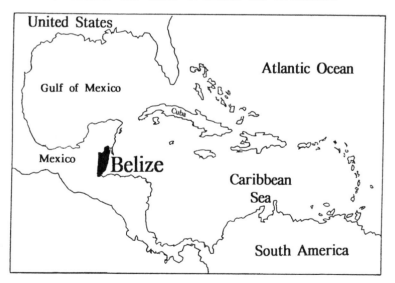

BELIZE

Chapter 5

The Lay of the Land

Belize is 180 miles long and 75 miles wide, with a land mass of 8,866 square miles (22,700 sq. kilometers). It is slightly larger than the state of Massachusetts.

If you think that's small, wait until you hear what the population is: 220,000. El Salvador is slightly smaller in size and has a population of over 6 million. So you begin to get the picture.

Small in size, true, but a land of tremendous variety. It's been said that there are many Belizes. From the beautiful sandy cayes (pronounced KEYS) with mile after mile of palm fringed beach, to the lush tropical rain forest of the South. Yes, Belize is small geographically, compared to other countries, but is doesn't seem so small when you live there. Realize, also that Belize is so underpopulated, that its landscape is still largely empty of human settlement. Unlike most Third World countries, Belize is without the huge overcrowded cities that generate pollution, filth and crime. It is as if most of Belize is untouched by human hands.

One thing about Belize: although there is a lot of sea coast, there is not much beach (sand) on the mainland.

The jungle grows right up to the sea.   And where there was beach in former times, they built towns on it, never imagining anyone would want to do anything as strange as take off most of their clothes and lay there in the sun.

Corozal

The northern most town in Belize is Corozal; only 9 miles from   the Mexican border.   It has a lovely seaside location and a population of around 8,500.   Corozal was founded by Mexican refuges in 1849 and was named after a type of palm tree.   In 1955, Hurricane Janet destroyed most of the town, which at that time consisted of adobe buildings and a historic fort.   Today, rebuilt Corozal is part Mexican style concrete-block houses and part Caribbean style clapboard homes, built up on stilts to catch the cool breeze coming off sparkling Corozal bay.

This is considered the "dry" region of the country with an annual rainfall between 50 to 60 inches.   The wet season here is from June to October, with some rain into January. Don't let any of that scare you off, rainfall is never a hindrance to doing anything here.

Much of the land around Corozal was cleared for raising sugar cane, the number one export.

Corozal has quite a few retired Canadians and Americans living in and around it. Some hang out at Nestor's Hotel and Restaurant #123   5th Ave. (Tel. 04-22354).   Nestor's is a good place to eat gringo food and an adequate, "bare bones" place to stay.   A lot of North Americans also hang around Hailey's Restaurant and Caribbean Village. It's a combination trailer park, campground and motel.   The setting is park-like and it's right on the bay, though their rates are a bit steep.   It's $20 single and $25 double to rent one of the modest Mayan-style thatched huts with all the cold water you can stand. To camp it's $5 per person per night; you provide your own tent or hammock. To park your RV it's $5 for the first person and $2.50 for each additional individual -- that's for self-contained.   With hookups, it's $8.75, and $5 per extra person. (Tel. 04-22725)

There is another campground up at 4-mile lagoon, near the border. It's much more rustic, but in a quieter setting. Look for the tottering sign that says "Lagoon Campground" it's on the left hand side about 3 miles down the road from the border. You don't need reservations at either of the trailer parks, just show up, you'll get a space. With the Lagoon campground you may have trouble finding the American owner, he's gone a lot of the time.

Consejo

Consejo is 7 miles northeast of Corozal. A taxi ride out there is around $10. Consejo is worth the trip. There are two parts to Consejo. One is Consejo Village, where native Belizeans live and the other is Consejo Shores, a Canadian development with fine homes built by mostly North Americans. There are waterfront lots for sale and a few houses for rent, but they are out of our $450 a month, price range. But, by U.S., standards you might not consider them that expensive. Bill Wildman is the name of the fellow running things out there. (Tel. 04-12005)

Sarteneja

This tiny picturesque fishing village is snuggled against an emerald bay, just around the point from Corozal. It's 30 minutes by boat or 4½ hours by road. Venus Bus line serves Sarteneja daily from Orange Walk.

This village is famous throughout Belize for its hand crafted fishing boats. A few isolated Americans live here on and off again. One day while taking pictures of men working on their boats, I was surprised to see 2 gringo girls working on a small fishing boat. They had bought their handsome 21 footer for $900 the year before in Sarteneja. They immediately headed for the cayes, but hit some bad weather along the way. And they had experienced a lot of trouble maneuvering every time their cotton sails got wet.

Now after refitting her with Dacron sails and sheets, they're exploring every island and caye in Belize and the Western Caribbean.

Be sure to visit the butterfly farm at Shipstern, just south of Sarteneja a bit, and slightly off the main road.

Copper Bank

On your way to Sarteneja you will pass the turnoff for Copper bank, Chunox, and Progresso. Check out the Progresso Lagoon, it's picture-postcard perfect. If you happen to make it all the way out to this remote area, be sure and look up Mrs. Anne Lowe in Copper Bank. She's a retired American Professor of something or other, from Washington D.C. She has lived in Belize for years, and now runs a small bed and breakfast called the Blue Heron Lagoon Resort. Cabanas rent for $30 a night. We assume meals are included, because there's no place to eat out there. Mrs. Lowe has a personality that won't quit and she'll talk your ear off on just about any subject pertaining to Belize.

Orange Walk

Orange Walk Town is 28 miles south of Corozal. With a population of 10,000 it is one of the largest towns in Belize. It is the sugar cane capital. The main sugar mill for the entire country is located just south of town. Trucks loaded with cane wait 24 hours or more in mile long lines, stringing out in all four directions.

Most of Belize's Mennonites live in this vicinity. But at about the distance of a day's ride out of town--by horse.

Frankly, you probably won't be spending a lot of time in Orange Walk. It has all the flavor of a rough and ready, Wild West town--with some of the same problems too. Although we have some retired friends who live there, we can't figure out why. It doesn't have much to attract most

1. Xuanantunich   2. Beautiful Corozal Bay

1.

1. Caye Caulker
2. Typical bush house
(not so typical paint job, by an American artist).

2.

1.

2.

3.

4.

5.

1. Ferry at
San Esteban
2. Belize City
Central Market
3. Belizean
lobster
4. Wood-carver
Raymond Guy
5. Ruins at
Santa Rita

1.

1. Juan Palomo, Belizean fruit vendor
2. An American family enjoying their seaside home

2.

of us foreigners. There are many larger archaeological sites nearby, and it's used as a home base by archaeologists working there.

Crooked Tree

About one half hour south of Orange Walk you'll see a sign for Crooked Tree. This quiet little village is located on an island at the end of a 3-mile causeway; in the middle of one of Central America's foremost bird sanctuaries. Ideal for nature lovers, but not much in the way of available housing.

Belmopan

The "new" Capital is at the geographic center of the country. The old capital of Belize City was destroyed by hurricanes on two different occasions. No sooner had they finished rebuilding it after the first one when the second one came along. The first hurricane happened in 1931 and the second in 1961. Belmopan is one of those "fake" capitals, although all government offices are located here, the cultural and commercial capital is still Belize City.

Belmopan is a completely planned city, neat, organized, and all cement. No wood structures are allowed. It stands in stark contrast to the rest of the country. You can live pretty well in Belmopan. There are some nice cement houses, reminiscent of tract homes built in the early 50's.

There's just not a lot of excitement here. As the young people say: "They no clubs here." Meaning night life and loud music are almost nonexistent here. You may consider that either an advantage or a disadvantage. Being so far inland, it tends to get hotter in the day and cooler at night than on the coast.

Most all of the 4,000 inhabitants of Belmopan live there because they have well paying government jobs. This is reflected in the price of rentals. Be prepared to pay twice as much for a house here, as other parts of the country.

Cayo

Continuing west from Belmopan, you'll come to the town of El Cayo de San Ignacio, called Cayo for short. San Ignacio is in a valley; and around it you'll see lush, green mountains, and cascading waterfalls.

There is a huge suspension bridge connecting San Ignacio with Santa Elena, it's sister town. This is the Hawkesworth Bridge, the longest suspension bridge in Central America. Some are awed by it. . . and some of us, it just makes nervous.

The combined population of the two towns is around 7,000. We find that Americans who come to Belize from the Midwest usually settle in Cayo. Here too, the slight increase in altitude, makes Cayo hotter in the day and cooler at night.

Actually, Cayo has quite an assortment of foreigners living there. This makes for some interesting restaurants and even a few health food stores.

When you get to Cayo, be sure to go to Eva's Restaurant and Bar. Just ask anyone where it is. Eva's is also the San Ignacio Tourist Information Center. You can eat there, use the phone, and find out everything you ever wanted to know about life in Belize. Eva's is the gathering place for *Belizers.* (What the locals call Gringo people who like Belize)

If for no other reason, go there just to hear the Cockney accent of Bob, the British fellow who runs Eva's. He's one of the more memorable characters you'll meet in this neck of the woods. He also can be quite helpful.

"Remo" Dan's Sandcastle is getting to be a real Gringo-hangout, known for its vegetarian pizza and 3 open walls overlooking the Macal River.

Dangriga

Dangriga is also know as Stann Creek. This place reminds me of a mini Belize City, population 8,000. This is the only other place besides Belize City where I would say you have to watch your purse, camera, and bags very closely, Be that as it may, we have American friends who love living here. They live in a nice location right on the sea. (There's even lots of sand on this beach).

This is mainly a Garifuna settlement. They celebrate their arrival here from Honduras in 1823 every November 19, with lots of drums, drinks, dancing, and gett'en down. The name Dangriga means "Standing Waters" in Garifuna. They even have their own flag.

Sunkist bought land here and planted oranges and grapefruits. The citrus industry is booming here. . . well as booming as any industry can get in Belize.

Placencia

Here is one place in Belize with actual beach. And what a beach it is! Fifteen miles of what looks like a South Sea Island, but is really a peninsula. It's connected to land about 100 road miles south of Belize City, just off the Southern Highway.

Surrounded by water on both sides--the Caribbean on its east and the Placencia lagoon on its west--the white sandy beach of this idyllic peninsula is lined for miles with beautiful palm trees, and not a soul in sight between villages.

Placencia used to be mainly a Garifuna, fishing village, but some savy Americans capitalized on the fantastic location and opened some exclusive resorts, with exclusive prices, of course. But there are also some affordable beach houses for rent in the center of Placencia Village. But don't expect to find them if you go house hunting in the middle of high season. Locals and North Americans living here pay rents that are a fraction of what the tourist pays for his 1 or 2 week stay in the "South Seas."

If you want to go to Placencia from Mango Creek, the going price is $15 a head. That's not bad, considering it takes about $15 of fuel to go there and back. When locals want of cross over, they go down to the "bridge" (dock) and wait for a local boat heading that way. The "local" price will range from 50 cents to $5, depending on who, when, and how many are going. Sorry, but you won't get this price, if you have lots of bags and look like a tourist.

Mango Creek

Mango Creek and Independence are twin towns adjacent to each other and directly across the lagoon from Placencia. There's a few Americans living here and very inexpensively too. They say it's because they can't find anything to spend their money on, in either Mango Creek or Independence. Canned goods are readily available in town but good vegetables are in short supply. In a places like Mango Creek we suggest growing a small garden to fill the need. (See our special report: *Gringo Gardening...How to Garden in Belize & Grow Food in the Tropics*)

Big Creek

This small town just south of Mango Creek is turning into an important deep-water port. Large shipments of bananas and tropical fruit leave here every week bound for England. It has the look of an Australian town in the out-back. There's one small trading center, one restaurant, one pub, one hotel, one bank, (open only on Friday), and one dusty air-strip. Throw in lots of Gringo plantation owners--this little place has charm.

Burrell Boom

This is a quiet little agricultural community on the way to

the Baboon Sanctuary at Bermudian Landing. Did I say quiet? I forgot about the black howler monkeys who serenade the neighborhood in the morning and just before they go to bed at night. I've also heard them howl right before a big rain storm--but never seen one.

You can rent a boat and take a tour of the sanctuary from a transplanted American couple living here. A small pocket of Gringos live along the river, and you'll understand why after you've seen Burrell Boom. It's the kind of place you'd expect to see Huck Finn come floating down the river at any moment.

Punta Gorda

Punta Gorda is the last town of any significant size in Belize. Population 3,000. It's about 200 road miles from Belize City; situated near the Guatemalan border, and sitting on the beautiful Gulf of Honduras.

P.G., (as the locals call it) started out as an isolated fishing village. Now it seems almost cosmopolitan--for Belize. There are a lot of Peace Corps workers and also the V.O.A. (Voice of America) installation for Central America is here. Even though P.G., is very isolated, you can get things here that are not to be found elsewhere in Belize: Fresh baked cinnamon rolls, whole wheat bread, homemade ice cream, and believe it or not, pizza with real mozzarella.

These businesses, all run by Americans and Canadians, have sprung up to cater to the tastes of all the foreigners living in P.G.

Punta Gorda is in true tropical rain forest territory, with 160 to 200 inches of rain per year--it's not as bad as it sounds. Like mythical Camelot it usually rains at night and you almost always wake up to clear skies. It can get pretty muddy--it's true, but don't imagine people paddling down the streets in canoes.

At one time you could rent a house in P.G., dirt cheap, but those days are gone--with all the Peace Corps and V.O.A., workers here now, the demand is great, driving up the price. You can still find something reasonable in town; however, it's just harder.

P.G., is in the Toledo District. About 130 years ago this district was populated with Americans. During the Civil War, Britain gave Americans fleeing the South free land. What happened to all those Americans? Where did their descendants go?. . . Ask the locals about them, and they have no idea what you're talking about. . . If you find out let us know.

Nim Li Punit is a ruin outside of P.G, at mile 75 of the Southern Highway. It's only one of many unrestored Mayan ruins in the area. It's in a great setting: Huge trees over head, giant vines--you'll feel like you're on the set of a Tarzan movie. Oh yeah. . . try not to gawk when the local Mayan women come out to sell trinkets--they walk around topless at home.

The road to P.G., is pretty rugged and in the wet season may be impassable. You can fly there via Maya Air.

Ambergris Caye

The largest of the 176 cayes scattered off the coast of Belize is also the most populated and developed. Ambergris is separated from Mexico by only a narrow channel (dug by Belize). The area was once claimed by Mexico. Spanish is spoken here more than English among the locals.

San Pedro is the island's biggest town. (Population 2,000) In the past few years San Pedro has experienced explosive growth. The once quiet sandy streets are now filled with taxis and ATV's whizzing by. This is the most touristy place in Belize. It has become the hideaway for European Jet-Setters and was even featured on "Lifestyles of the Rich and Famous." There are many ultra-expensive hotels here that cater to this crowd. Unfortunately all this has raised the price of everything. Especially rent and it's no longer affordable for the average retiree on a fixed income. Some of our friends living here, have had to tighten their belts to keep up with these changes.

Too bad, because the palms were inviting, the beaches were great and the reef was fantastic. But San Pedro isn't the only place like this, also there is. . .

Caye Caulker

Here is your basic affordable tropical island paradise. South of Ambergris and only about 20 miles from Belize City by sea or air. Its population of around 800 is quite a blend: Belizean lobster fishermen, and their families mix with artists, retirees, back-packers, and general hippie types from all over the world.

The beaches here are littered with enormous, glistening pink, and purple conch shells. There are only 3 cars on the whole island; and affordable housing is available (a small beach house rents for around $200 a month).

There are 2 great places to eat here, that you would never be able to find by yourself. Ask for Sid's or Glenda's. Both restaurants are run out of private homes. They aren't open all the time, but when they are you can get big, fat lobster burritos for $1 (when in season). For desert walk down to Reina Patt's and try a mouth watering pie or homemade banana cake, hot out of the oven.

The airstrip is finally in and served by daily flights. To get to Caye Caulker by boat: Catch the Triple-J or one of the other boats at the Swing Bridge or the nearby Shell station in Belize City. They leave every morning at 8:30. The cost is $11 per person round trip, and the hour long trip is more like a sightseeing tour of the cays. To get back to Belize City from Caye Caulker (perish the thought) just ask around, boats go every morning at 7 a.m.; or catch the

Triple-J on her return trip at 3:30 p.m. daily, from the Rainbow bridge (dock).

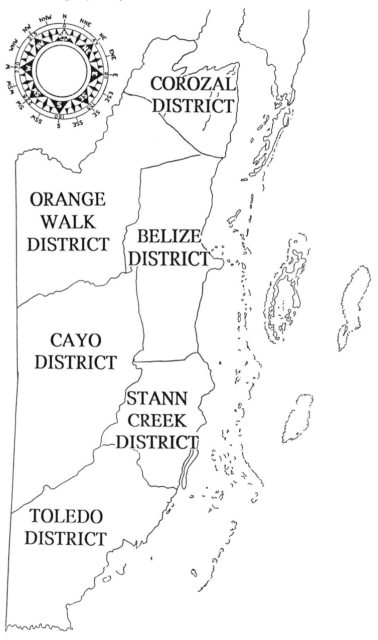

Chapter 6
Belize City

Settled 300 years ago by English pirates, Belize City is now a ramshackle mixture of decaying British colonialism and Caribbean culture.

Grip yourself, Belize City is the exact opposite of the rest of the country. Filled with 70,000 people, it's an overgrown shanty town. It's houses are wooden, sagging structures propped up on stilts, that can't even remember what color they used to be painted. It reminds us of the drawings in *Tom Sawyer*.

It started out as a temporary logging camp and pirate's lair. If anyone had known it was going to be around for this long, another location would have been chosen, as the disadvantages here are many. It's built on swamp, sand dunes and legend has it, rum bottles. Hanging out into the ocean, on a little spit of land, it's a prime target for hurricanes.

But what you'll notice more then the open sewers and canals that run through town, are the people. Belize City has the most bizarre cast of rip-off artists, con-men, and hucksters roaming its streets. And believe me, they can smell a tourist a mile away.

Belize City is legendary for its thieves. The legend is both exaggerated and at the same time well earned. Yes, it's incredibly easy to get ripped off in Belize. (When the locals say "Belize" they mean the city). Especially the first time you are there. But it is also easy to not get ripped off at all, it all depends on you.

If you look like an easy mark, chances are you'll be one. But follow the rules and you'll be all right, and maybe even actually enjoy Belize City. Yes enjoy, because for all of its faults, Belize City is a very colorful place. And in time it will grow on you and you may even get to like it.

Follow the same kind of rules you would in New York City: Don't carry anything loosely; bag, camera, purse. Ladies, keep that purse tucked under your arm and close to your body. Keep that camera in a bag and out of sight until you're ready to use it. . . then quickly put it away. Don't wear anything flashy. I suggest not wearing any jewelry at all. **Don't walk around at night**, even in pairs or small groups--take a taxi everywhere, even in the daytime this is best until you know the territory. Don't get involved with anyone you meet on the street, as sad as their story may sound. Don't go anywhere with anyone you don't know.

And try not to act frightened if some extremely skinny, toothless, and wild-eyed fellow with hair like a tube sponge comes up and tells you Haile Selassie is alive. He's only a "Rasta" (Rastafarian) and it's part of his religion to do that sort of thing. . . He may try to sell you drugs. . . . that's part of his religion too.

Once a woman followed my mother-in-law through the old market in Belize City, she was being very friendly--too friendly. Tenderly, she put her arm around my mother-in-law's shoulder, then gingerly began fingering the chain around her neck. . . suddenly, she realized it was a medical alert tag and not 18k gold. She abruptly left.

If you step off the bus with a $750 camera dangling from your shoulder loosely, it may be only seconds before it's gone--really. There's an unknown number of people in this little community who's "job" is. . . to get up every morning and look for something to "thieve." Fathers have proudly passed this "trade" on to their sons, since the pirate days. Be determined you're not going to be victimized here. Have a positive, purposeful attitude, and don't ever cower or act afraid.

The fellow who approaches you on the street, and tries to force you to let him carry your bags to the hotel his cousin owns 3 blocks away, isn't the same as the mugger in New York City. Although they may look the same to you. These people by nature aren't as vicious as "our muggers" back in the U.S. Guns are seldom used to commit crimes-- but we've noticed that with the arrival of cable-TV, American style crime is increasing in Belize, as impressionable young people try out things they've seen in the movies. (Can you imagine drive-by shootings from a bicycle and a homemade gun?) Remember, guns are outlawed in Belize, even the police don't carry them. For the most part these street larcenists just want to run off with your bag, not kill you.

Be firm, Belizeans are very mellow people, they don't like aggression, it scares them. When they up and get in your face, bark back at them! "Leave me alone! Don't touch my bag!" If someone runs by and grabs for your camera don't let them take it, grab it back! (Don't you wish you could do this in New York City?) Be assertive, that'll scare them off most of the time.

I will never forget the first time I was in Belize City, We had way too much luggage, more than we could carry. (Bill was bringing down car parts for a friend). We instantly became the target, of offers to "help" with our bags.

One of us would have to stand guard over the luggage, while the other went to find out about the bus. I learned quickly that I had to be firm and forceful with these characters.

Finally Bill returned with our bus tickets, and we began to edge our pile towards the bus. Just then a man approached, reaching for a bag he asked: "Are you going to be traveling on this bus?"

I spun around and said: (as if I had grown up on New York subways).

"Put that bag down!"

"But Miss, you don't understand, I'm trying to help you."

I'd heard this line all day. "Put it down, now!"

This time I sounded like Clint Eastwood, low key, but very forceful. My eyes narrowed as I stared the tall man down. "Drop the bag." I was getting good at this.

"But I'm the bus driver and we're loading the baggage compartment, Mum."

"Oops, sorry."

But it's OK to hate Belize City and still love Belize. Many people do. In fact, you can live in Belize and never go to Belize City at all. At times, we've gone months, and months without once stepping foot in the place. Belizeans from the villages don't like to go there either. One night, our Belizean neighbors had a medical emergency. They asked us to drive them in their family truck to Belize City; because, they'd never been there, and had no idea where the hospital was.

Don't worry, the rest of the country is nothing like Belize City. It is calm, peaceful, rural, and the people are humble and hard working. On the other hand, Belize City is crowded, and congested, with people living on top of each other. I suppose that's why people act so differently there.

Now, after all this, you may go there and have no problems at all. Good. We hope that's the case, but we would rather you be prepared than not.

Some friends from the States came to visit. They wanted to take the bus and go into Belize City for the day. We were unable to accompany them, but warned them what to expect beforehand. Upon their return that night we wondered what wild tales they would have to tell.

"Well, how was it?" we asked.

"Fine," they replied.

"Fine?" we asked, almost disappointed.

"Yeah, we're from Chicago remember, that Belize City is nothing to us."

Some say the worst thieves in Belize are the ones driving taxi cabs. The fares are regulated, but they do try and take advantage of foreigners, I'll admit.

The best way not to get ripped off by a cab driver in Belize City is to ask someone, really anyone who lives there, what the fare is supposed to be. They will tell you, and when you approach a taxi driver, you tell him where you want to go, and how much the fare is.

"I want to go to Brodies, it's $5 Belize, right?"

They might try to tell you it's more; or that it's $5 American; that's a trick they use all the time, especially on the way to and from the airport. But stand your ground, you may have to try more than one taxi cab to get the real price. Expect to pay $1 Belize extra per person, if you're traveling in a group.

Another form of "robbery" in Belize City is hotel gouging. You're paying for a safe location here, rather than luxury or even comfort, and pay you will!

The first time we were here, an acquaintance said he knew of a safe place to stay, near the police station. He got us to the hotel just as night fell. We felt we had no other choice but to pay the $44 U.S., for a stink hole of a room. Then to add insult to injury, we had to pay $16 U.S., apiece for a meal that would have only been $4 anywhere else in town.

Safe, clean, decent places to stay in Belize City are few and far between--a few of them are: Seaside Guest House,

(#3 Prince Street, Tel. 02-78339). It was getting a bit run down and overrun with chain-smoking European back-packers, until some Quakers took it over. This is still the best bargain in Belize City, with rooms about $15. You'll have to share a bathroom though.

Nicer and still reasonable are Colton House, (#9 Cork Street, Tel. 02-44666) and Fort Street Guest House, (#4 Fort Street, Tel. 02-30116/ fax 02-78808). If you can afford to stay at the Belize Biltmore (Mile 3, Northern Highway, Tel. 02-32302/ fax 02-32301) it's like staying at a nice motel in the U.S., with air-conditioning, telephone, TV, and pool. It's location is great. It's close to the airport, close enough to Belize City to be convenient but far enough out of town to be safe. It's about $70 a night though, for single or double. (For more sage advice on where to stay and not stay in Belize City see our special report: *Bill & Claire's Hotel and Restaurant Guide to Belize.*)

Belize City is like a Tennesse Williams play, gone Creole. Everyone you meet is a character, larger than life. Enjoy yourself, soak up the atmosphere--and watch your camera.

Hand cranked Swing Bridge, Belize City

Chapter 7
The People

Belize really is a melting pot. Belizeans come in every shade and color. I remember when I first went to Belize thinking: "Is this person black? or white? Mexican? or Chinese?" Actually they were probably all of the above, they were Belizean.

The largest group of people and the ones who are most thought of as Belizean are the Creoles. Creoles are a smooth blend of Scottish pirates and African slaves. They also come in all shades of the rainbow. Most Creoles look to us like Black Americans. Don't call them black. Don't call anyone in Belize black. It can be very insulting to them. Creoles don't consider themselves black.

In Belize only the Garifuna are considered black. These are the Caribs: A mix of Carib Indian women from South America, and runaway African slaves. They prefer to use their African name Garinagu. At first North Americans can't tell a Creole person apart from a Garifuna; except that the Garifuna are generally more African looking. The Garifuna people are proud of their heritage and speak their African language, as well as Spanish, English, and sometimes Mayan. They live mostly in Southern Belize, particularly around Dangriga and the coast.

At one time I thought that there were a lot of Mexicans and Guatemalans living in Belize, not so. These are the people called in Creole, "Belize Spanish" the Mestizos. They are of Yucatecan and Guatemalan descent. Many live in the Corozal, Orange Walk, and Cayo districts. They prefer to speak Spanish. Many of them are farmers raising sugar cane among other crops. Their diet is slightly different-- for instance, they eat the delicious black beans that Creoles usually won't touch.

The Maya were the first inhabitants of what is now called Belize. They make up about 10% of the population today. There are three distinct groups of Maya: The Yucatecan, the Mopan, and the Ketchi. Each has their own language, not understood by the other.

The Maya are tiny people (the women are about the size of a   10 year old child). They are distinguished by their thick black hair, almond shaped eyes, and high cheek bones.

Their life style is sometimes quite primitive. In the South, they often live in a thatched pole house, with dirt floors and a fire-pit for cooking. Many of these houses are without running water or electricity.

The women go about the village wearing no tops, grinding corn, and beating laundry on rocks. You really feel like you've gone back in time--until you look through the doorway of a thatched hut, and see the glow of a portable TV set, intricately hooked up to an old car battery.

Some in Belize call themselves Hindu, or Coolie. They are Belizeans of East Indian descent.

And also you will come across assorted Lees, Quans and other Belizeans of Chinese lineage. If you ask them if they're Chinese, they'll probably say "no," as they consider "Chinese" only those who are just now immigrating from Taiwan, Hong Kong, and Mainland China. These new Chinese emigrants are usually the proprietors of small shops, restaurants and "Fry Chicken" stands. You'll also see a sprinkling of Lebanese throughout the country.

An interesting addition to this crazy quilt is the Mennonites. They are a religious sect, similar to the Amish. In fact, the Amish broke away from the Mennonites in the 17th Century. They're of German descent and had been living in Canada, until they moved to Chihuahua, Mexico to escape mechanization. However, in the late 1950's they realized Mexico was becoming too modern; and after the government started interfering with the education of their children they immigrated to Belize, with the help of Emory King.

The men dressed in denim bib-overalls, straw hats, huarache sandals; and the women in print dresses, and bonnets, are a common sight.

The Mennonites make furniture, grow crops, raise poultry and run dairy farms. Everything they produce is of the highest quality. They remain quite isolated, by choice and language. They speak Plattdeutsch, an archaic Low German dialect and Spanish, but usually no English.

The gene pools are so strong among the Mennonites that they all look alike to us. I thought I was seeing the same young Mennonite woman over and over again, but in different parts of the country.

One would think that since Belize is next door to Mexico and Guatemala that the people would be very similar. I discovered that wasn't the case, the minute I stepped onto my first Batty's bus in Chetumal. I could feel the difference, and see it, on the faces of the passengers.

Belizeans in general are quiet, introverted people--by our standards. Most of them quite shy, and bashful, not as animated as their Mexican neighbors. Of course there are exceptions to the rule, but they are generally very low key. Although they can be very kind and hospitable, don't expect the same larger than life: "Mi casa, es su casa," welcome the Latino culture gives you.

Having just written that, I recall a time we were walking down a dusty street in Cayo. A very old, leathery skinned couple passed us on the street. As they recognized we were foreigners the woman came up, kissed me on both cheeks and said: Welcome to Belize" then continued on her way down the street.

1995 or 1895?
Mennonite horsecarts near Camp One,
Shipyard, Orange Walk District

Chapter 8
Living In Belize

Food

Because of isolation, bad roads, and a negative attitude in the past toward raising crops, Belize has not had a great variety of commodities available. There were parts of the country where people lived on canned food and staples. Rice and beans have been the mainstay since the days when pirates turned woodcutters, had to transport dry foods to logging camps deep in the interior.

Things are much better today. A diverse selection of foods are always available at the market: Cabbage, tomatoes, cucumbers, onions, potatoes, carrots, celery, jicama, chiles, sweet peppers (local name for bell pepper), cauliflower, plantains, and sweet potato. Available occasionally or seasonally are sweet corn, lettuce, and avocados (that are four inches across and taste like butter). Fruits always available are: Papaya, many varieties of banana, sweet oranges, sour oranges, sweet lemons (similar to grapefruit), limes, custard-apples, guava, sapodilla, mamey apples, golden plums, and seasonally those delicious sweet mangoes. Keep in mind that when you shop here, produce is fresh-- vine ripened--unheard of in U.S. supermarkets.

Corn tortillas are sold in tortillerias on practically every corner. Made fresh while you wait, you get them hot off the press. Let me add that in certain parts of the country, where there are not a lot of Mestizos there are few or no tortillerias. Flour tortillas although they are commonly eaten, are not available in stores and must be made at home. You can always get a neighbor lady to make you a batch for a small price. Unfortunately white "Wonder" type bread is the norm, and whole wheat is hard to find. (You can get whole wheat bread in Belize City, Cayo, and Punta Gorda.) Whole wheat flour is also available in "supermarkets" everywhere.

You can get excellent quality chicken country-wide thanks to the Mennonites who grow and market poultry under the names *Caribbean Chicken* and *Quality Chicken.* The label that reads in Belize Creole: "Dis da fi we chicken" (This is our chicken) is from the blond haired, blue eyed business savvy Mennonites. You can also get fresh chicken from many Mom and Pop places. By fresh we mean it's walking around in the yard when you order it. Thirty minutes later, you're handed a warm bag of chicken--plucked and cleaned of course. Beef and pork are readily available, dressed fresh each day (we know, we used to live across the street from the slaughter house!). Meats are available in the market till about noon.

The seafood is wonderful; red snapper, black snapper, barracuda, conch, shrimp, crab, lobster--all are abundant and cheap compared to U.S. prices.

The waters of Belize are teeming with fish; locally we noticed an overabundance of catfish; but Belizeans won't eat them. They have very strong feelings about certain foods. It's best not to try and talk them into changing their minds. We regularly catch our own catfish and enjoy eating them very much.

If a Belizean sees you with a catfish, he will in all sincerity try to talk you out of eating such a "dirty fish." The local fishermen may be even more "vocal." So, just thank them and explain that you're catching these for your pet cat (Puss will have to fight me for my fried Catfish!).

Gary an American friend living in Dangriga, liked to catch catfish near the bridge in town. The towns folk would constantly scold him for eating "dirty fish"--then bend down and draw up drinking water from the exact same spot where Gary was catching his "dirty fish."

We went fishing with two Mayan friends once. Each time they found a catfish in their net, they flew into a rage; grabbed the thing and flung it as far away as they could-- big fat juicy ones, so many I lost count. After a long day of fishing, we came back home with a boat load of tiny, little silver fish--about the size of a sardine. . . they couldn't have been happier.

There's lots of other fish too. Our friend Leo keeps a fish trap made of chicken wire over the side of his boat at all times--he catches more fish than he can eat. Each time he cleans a fish he puts the guts back inside the trap as bait.

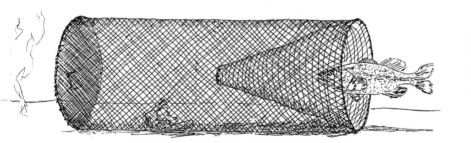

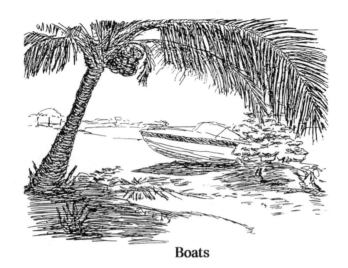

Boats

If you live in Belize and own a boat . . . the quality of life's little pleasures and the amount of fish you can eat increases dramatically. The size of your boat doesn't matter, it can be just big enough for you and the little-woman or maybe only yourself.

You don't have to be rich to own a boat and you don't have to be a nautical genius to build one, just determined. There was a time when boatbuilding was an American heritage, and every red blooded American knew how to make his own skiff, dory, or rowboat, with simple hand tools.

Nowadays that's a forgotten legacy--except for places like Belize. Plus it's easier with today's power tools, and Belize has some of the best hardwoods for boatbuilding in the world. All you need is the know-how. Where do you get that? Belizeans pass it on from father to son. But we found some excellent old, and often out-of-print boat-building books, at library sales and second hand stores. *(23 Boats You Can Build* by Popular Mechanics is a classic). We knew we were promising sailors; but didn't know a thing about boatbuilding, and couldn't tell a sheer from a chine. But now that we've got a couple of small boats under our belt, our fingers are itching to try something bigger.

You could bring a boat with you, but we wouldn't recommend pulling a boat trailer thru Mexico; and the duty on a boat that size is around 40% when you cross the Belizean border. So you might consider building your own or bringing something small enough to strap on your car.

Eating Out

So you'll know what you're eating, here's a primer on Belizean foods:

Johnny Cakes are very similar to the biscuits eaten in the American South. *Fry Jacks* are flour tortillas fried crisp sprinkled with a little sugar or salt. *Salbutes* and *garnachas* are corn tortillas fried crisp, with refried beans, shredded chicken, chopped cabbage and tomatoes, a little grated cheese on top, and finished off with habanero chiles. Both are like a little tostada. These are Belizean snacks. . . fast-food.

Warning: Beware of the habanero. This chile, used so freely here, is said to be the hottest in the world. Consider it armed and dangerous. If you're wary of hot spicy foods . . . stay away from it.

Scientifically the "hotness" of a chile pepper is measured in what are called *Scoville units.* Jalapeño peppers register at 5,000 Scoville units. The habanero is somewhere between 200,000 and 300,000 Scoville units.

My first experience with a habanero was when a friend asked me to chop one for salsa. Little did I know that rubber gloves were required. It actually burned the skin off my fingertips. I even rubbed my eye before I realized what had happened.

These are usually served separately in a little jar on the table of the restaurant and are generally not mixed in with the food (you can always request that your food be prepared without chile).

Habaneros are usually served on top of both garnachas and salbutes. You'll see a bottle of orange sauce on tables everywhere in Belize. This is habanero sauce, use it sparingly at first, if at all. These things make jalapeños seem like jelly beans, that's why the Maya call it the "crying tongue."

Because Belizeans do not have a history of dining out; they are just starting to learn the ropes of the restaurant business. But, you can find some good restaurants, even great ones, if you know what to look for. We are currently eating our way though Belize researching the first ever restaurant guide to Belize. (See it listed in the Resources section)

A Chinese restaurant usually won't disappoint you. They even seem to have more variety than some in the U.S. (conch chow mein, and lobster chop suey, for example) even if you don't like Chinese food they can probably whip up something to please you. . . Just ask.

The only Mennonite restaurants we know of are in "Spanish Lookout," up in the Cayo district. They're open from 11 a.m. till 2 p.m. and are never open on weekends. Friendly Family Foods, or "Triple F" as it's called, is a restaurant, food store, and candy factory combined. Be sure and try their chocolate peanut brittle.

There are some American run restaurants country-wide and most are very good. If you eat in a Belizean owned restaurant, you can't go wrong ordering the national dish: "Rice and Beans" (not to be confused with beans and rice, which is a different meal entirely). It's much tastier than it sounds. The rice is cooked in coconut milk, and red kidney beans are added sparingly. A big mound of this is served next to a piece of Belizean stewed chicken, a scoop of "vegetable salad" (actually potato salad) and a strip of fried plantain. Douse this with some habanero sauce and you're in business.

Escabeche is another winner. It's a soup made with chicken and a lot of onions--kind of vinegary and spicy hot. Most Gringos love it. (For more information see our Special Report: *Cooking/Eating in Belize*)

Pets

There are certain medical papers you must have before you'll be allowed to bring your pet into Belize. One is proof of inoculation against rabies, the other is a veterinarian certification of good health. Be sure you have these. They are real sticklers for details in this area.

Contact the Belizean Consulate/Embassy:
2535 Massachusetts Ave., N.W., Washington, D.C., 20008 or phone (202) 332-9636 for the necessary forms and any additional requirements.

Crime

Petty theft is the biggest problem you may have to deal with living in Belize. The thieves aren't as vicious as up North, but they are very clever. And they think that all us North Americans are rich, because we have so many "things." To the average Belizean the amount of "stuff" the average North American needs to live is staggering.

You don't have to live in fear of being attacked, they just want to sneak in when you're not at home and steal your stereo. So be sure your house is secured! Have shutters or bars on the windows. It's amazing how small of a space these thieves can fit through; it makes me think they're all some kind of skinny, acrobatic-contortionists.

An excellent form of protection against petty theft is a dog. The bigger and louder the better. Belizeans are deathly afraid of dogs. Because of some sort of super-stition, black dogs of any breed or size are especially terrifying.

Don't think we're being overly paranoid about the "thieving" --anything not nailed down is going to disappear. Certain parts of Belize City are really the only areas you have to worry about personal safety, but theft is common everywhere.

Health

Let's just preface this section by saying that we're fairly paranoid in this area of our life. Most people come to Belize drink the water, eat the food, sleep without a mosquito net and have no problems at all. They laugh at us; as we filter our rain water, or wash our eating utensils with alcohol (at restaurants). Be that as it may, here are our recommen-dations:

The tap water is treated and safe to drink. Tap water is called "pipe water" in Belize, and one drink will tell you why. . . it tastes like an old pipe. Most people drink rain water, which is collected in a "vat" outside their house. Because of possible contamination in your rain gutter (i.e. bird droppings or a dead mouse) you need to purify your rain water in some way. You can either boil it for 20 minutes (rapidly); add Clorox to it--about 4 drops per gallon and let it stand for thirty minutes before drinking (some put it out in the sun all day to get rid of the Clorox taste). Food grade hydrogen peroxide can be used in the same way; or you can filter your drinking water. You'll need a filter that's good for bacteria, not just taste. We travel with a portable filter called "First Need." The cost is around $50 and the filter is available at any camping store. We got our "First Need " filter through REI Commercial Sales: 1700 45th St. Sumner, WA 98390 Tel. 1-800-426-

4840. But consider bringing down something more permanent when you move, or boil your water like we do.

While there are certain tropical diseases that exist here, Belize seems to be a perfect antidote for the common health problems of retirement age folks: High blood pressure, over-weight, arthritis, heart problems. The sunshine, clean air, exercise, fresh food, and lack of stress seem to do wonders for these problems.

You don't encounter the same health risks here that you do in other Third World countries. Belize is a cut above in cleanliness. The British, it seems, taught them about water treatment and septic tanks. It is still possible to get sick here, but it's much easier to stay healthy. Follow the same practices you do in Mexico and you'll be just fine.

Although Malaria does exist in Belize, doctors in the U.S. tend to over react and prescribe preventive doses of Chloroquine for anyone going to Belize, even for a two-week vacation.

Yet, what everyone seems to overlook is the fact that taking quinine is not the number one prevention against malaria: Sleeping with a mosquito net over your bed is!

It is much wiser and healthier to do this, than take the drug. Besides you can't take the pills forever. Two years is the maximum. After that it can damage your liver and then if you ever did get malaria, the drug wouldn't work for you.

Using a net may sound strange, and terribly tropical at first, but it's quite simple and easy to get used to. You may have trouble finding a net--especially a good one, that's not just decorative. Try shops in "Chinatown," if you live in a big city. Also try stores like *Pier 1 Imports*. It's particularly hard to find one large enough for a king sized bed. Mosquito nets are all but impossible to find in Belize, but you can always get them in Chetumal; ask for a *pavion* (PAW VEE OWN).

True, you do have to get used to using a net, but once you do, it's no trouble. Some even think sleeping under a mosquito net is very romantic.

Today malaria is a curable disease.   We know some who have gotten it, took the medication right away and were fine the very next day; and they're still fine years later with no recurrence.

We've never heard of anyone who uses a net, getting malaria. There is little chance that you'll contact malaria in Belize at this time.   The government has a very stringent anti-malarial program. And as much as we don't like the malathion they spray, it's very effective.

Avoid dark clothing, wear long sleeves after dusk; cover your feet and ankles with shoes and socks when walking through deep grass and especially at night.

Before you rule out the notion of using a mosquito net entirely, consider this: In the tropics there are other tiny uninvited guests that may wander into your bedroom during the night.   A net will protect you from becoming strange bedfellows.

Health Care

It is easy enough to find a doctor or a hospital in Belize. Every town has a government run hospital as well as several private doctors to choose from. The care you get from these can range from abysmal to excellent.

You may feel you'll get better care with a private doctor; maybe you will. But we've gotten fine care from doctors at the government hospital and have had horrible experiences with private doctors. It's hard to call it.

An office visit with a private doctor is usually about $5 and prescriptions are a few dollars more. Everything at the government hospital or clinic is free; (even for a visitor) examinations, medication, and tests, but you'll notice a box where you can leave a donation.

There is emergency medical care available in Belize but, it isn't anything like we're used to; no trauma centers; no paramedics. We recommend that everyone have a comprehensive first aid kit on hand and learn CPR.

Mexico on the other hand, has excellent medical services available. We have used medical doctors, hospitals, chiropractors and dentists in Mexico and were very pleased.

If you wear contact lenses bring your supplies down with you, because they are hard to get in Belize. You can have them sent thru the mail. We do.

If you are currently taking medication, you'll be happy to know that you can usually get your prescriptions filled with the same drugs that you'd get in the States and at a reduced price too!

Many of you have written and asked if your insurance policies will cover you outside the United States. You need to ask your insurance carrier for that information; policies

will vary, some do, some don't. Don't assume yours won't.
You'll never know unless you ask them. You may be
surprised to find out your policy covers you anywhere in
the world--we were. Unfortunately, Medicare only covers
you in the U.S.

Clothes

The more cotton you have on, the more comfortable
you'll be. This has been a hard lesson for some to learn.
Especially for those who love their no-iron polyester. But
you've got to face facts: Wear polyester in the tropics and
you'll be stewing in your own juices.

Even poly/cotton blends are uncomfortable most of the
year. We recommend everything be 100% cotton or
another natural fiber like linen, silk, or even rayon (made
from wood) This includes underwear, bras, socks, etc.
Ladies, you won't have much need for stockings. You'll be
most comfortable in a cotton shift and a pair of sandals.

Belize is just now getting used to the idea of women
wearing shorts (but not too short). Culottes, or walking
shorts are fine. They're not thrilled with bathing suits for
women either. You can wear one, but be prepared for a lot
of unsolicited male attention, regardless of your age.

The local women go swimming (or bathing as they say) in
their street clothes. You'll do well in a tank top and shorts.
Men can wear a regular bathing suit with no problem, but
it's not acceptable to be anywhere without a shirt on, except
in the ocean swimming, or in the privacy of your own
home.

Comfortable, sturdy walking shoes are a must; preferably
ones with soles that have a good grip (tractor treads). Here
you care more about traction than fashion.

Entertainment

Television is now available everywhere in Belize, and we mean U.S. television: Local news from Denver, Geraldo Rivera, Joan Rivers. You can have cable T.V. installed for $12.50 a month and get everything; CNN, Discovery, Disney channel, HBO, the works.

Every town of any size has a video rental store. In our town it's located in the "lobby" of the local TV station, that's operated out of the owners house. The TV tower is in his front yard; and he sells pizza and hamburgers out of his wife's kitchen. So you might want to bring down your VCR with you.

Movie theaters are all but nonexistent in Belize. They were very popular until about 5 years ago when cable came along. After that most theaters went out of business. Movies are still shown now and again, but it's usually in an auditorium with folding chairs. And most films are generally dreadful B-grade movies of the Kung-Fu/Porno genre.

Shopping

This is not the great national past time, although you can get everything you need to live comfortably in the local shops. Your shopping is divided into 2 categories: The "market" and the "shops."

The market is usually held every morning in the open air, till about 1 or 2 p.m. There you'll find all your produce, meat, fish, and some staples like beans and rice.

There are also market stalls that do shoe repair, sell herbs (bush medicine) and cook hot food. The latter, are called "food-stalls" and you can get a snack or a complete hot meal to go. If you eat your meal at the food stalls, they have tables outside like an outdoor cafe.

The market is a social affair, as much as a chore. Some

shop everyday, because the food you buy is ripe, and won't last long. The market is meant to be enjoyed. Stroll along in the sunshine, or visit with your favorite fruit lady, or vegetable man. You'll probably end up doing most of your buying from the same person every time, and they'll show their appreciation by giving you good deals and freebies.

Shops

The shops are on just about every street corner, and they can be as simple as canned foods on two shelves in someone's living room, or a "mini-super" with a little bit of everything, including frozen chicken and meats.

Canned goods predominant; you'll find canned milk and even canned butter. Be sure to try some fresh Mennonite milk. Look for the Western Dairies blue and white carton. It's the most delicious milk we've ever tasted, and their cheese is good too!

Some things in the shops are outrageously expensive because they are imported and Belize charges a high import duty. It works like this:

The shopkeeper buys a bottle of shampoo for $1.25 wholesale. Normally he would resell it for $2.50 but since duty on cosmetic items is 100% he has to pay another $1.25 per bottle to bring it into the country. Now he has paid $2.50 for that bottle and has to sell it for $5 to make his profit. That's why you'll see a bottle of Johnson & Johnson Baby Shampoo selling for $5.

For this and other reasons, most Belizeans do their major shopping out of the country. Mention Chetumal, or Melchor and their eyes light up.

Belize is so small, that you're never far from a border, and both border towns of Chetumal, Mexico and Melchor de Mencos, in Guatemala cater to Belizean shoppers. Chetumal has modern shopping malls--Melchor doesn't.

You can save a lot once you learn what to buy outside of Belize.   We make a shopping trip once a month and stock up on soap, canned goods, cereal, and other things that are much cheaper in Chetumal. You can hop a Belizean bus to Chetumal and walk from the bus parking lot to the market a few feet away.

At times (it's arbitrary) you may have to pay some duty to bring your groceries into Belize, but it still pays to shop outside for certain items.   Find out which items are restricted before you go (a current list is always posted at the border).   I had my bottle of bleach confiscated at the border once, because they make bleach in Belize and you can't bring it in from Mexico (but from the U.S. is OK; figure that out). The Belizean government is very protective of Belizean made products.

Money

One of our biggest concerns before we moved down to Belize, was how we would handle financial matters, such as bank accounts, checks, changing currency, getting money from the U.S. to Belize, and vice-versa.

We imagined it would be so difficult. But it couldn't have been easier.   We saw what other Gringos did and wisely followed suit.   Yes, they have banks in Belize; Lloyds, Bank of Nova Scotia, Belize Bank, and Atlantic Bank, just to name a few.   Most foreigners living in Belize keep all but a small amount of their money in banks at home. . . you never know what may happen with foreign currencies. . . it could devalue overnight.   For example, if you had all of your savings converted into Belize dollars and then the currency was devalued you'd lose.   There's not much chance of this happening though. The Belize dollar has never been devaluated, ever.   The Belize dollar is backed by the British Pound; it's fixed at 2 to 1 against the American dollar and Canada underwrites all her banks.

If you're on Social Security, *Direct Deposit* to your U.S. account is all you need.   Then after you open an account with a Belizean bank, you can simply write checks on your U.S. checking account and have them cashed in Belize dollars. Keep a minimum balance in this account that will cover your monthly checks. Otherwise the bank will hold your checks 6 weeks before crediting it to your account.

An easy way to open a bank account in Belize is to use a Visa or a MasterCard cash advance. It will take 3 or 4 days to clear--this isn't much help in an emergency (but for a fee of $5 --payable in advance--the bank will fax your bank up north and give you same day service).

There is usually no need to deposit more than $500 U.S. in a Belizean bank.   Leave this amount alone, and never touch it. This will enable you to write checks on your U.S. or Canadian bank account and have them cashed instantly in Belizean currency.   Maintaining this amount should cover daily   expenses   and   most   emergencies,   allowing   you $1,000 BZ at a moment's notice.

The reason we suggest this small amount is: If for some reason you have to leave the country in a hurry. . . you'll receive your cash back in Belize dollars only.   The banks will not tell you this when you open your account. We've had friends who have had to leave unexpectedly, and it was the same story each time.   Late the night before they left, they were still running around--scrambling from friend to friend, pockets bulging with money--trying to find someone who could change all their Belize currency back into U.S. dollars.

You can "buy" American dollars from Belizean banks. But they have to get permission from the government if it's over $500 dollars, which takes time.   You also lose about 2% on the exchange.   Belize dollars cannot be changed anywhere outside Belize, not even Mexico, or Guatemala. So if you leave with Belize dollars, you're pretty much stuck with them.

"Belizean Dollars can't be changed outside the country!"

The Pesero

A Pesero is a professional money changer. This is a perfectly legal occupation. Peseros are honest hard working men and they are not out to cheat you. The Belize banking industry would like you to think that it's illegal to change money anywhere but in a bank. This is not true. There are no laws against money changing. They'd also like you to believe that a Pesero will rip you off. As of this writing a Pesero will pay you up to $2.05 BZ for every U.S. dollar, the banks only pay $1.98 BZ. Now who is trying to rip who off? (Bear in mind, that this rate fluctuates daily).

Ask around, find a Pesero you like, and do business with him regularly. Eventually, he'll cash your personal checks into Belize dollars for you.

As soon as you cross the border into Belize, Peseros will mob you--wanting to change U.S. dollars to Pesos; Pesos to Belize dollars--anything. Don't be afraid, that's just the way they do business. Peseros will cash your travelers checks for a higher rate of exchange than a bank.

If you're crossing at the Mexico/Belize border, ask the Peseros for Jose Sanchez. He's our favorite.

Transportation

There's good news and bad news. The good news is you can get along quite well without a car in Belize. The bad news is, should you choose to bring a car to Belize it's going to cost you.

Bus transportation is reliable and cheap, For example a bus trip from Belize City to Punta Gorda is 8 hours long and costs around $15. If you live near a main highway, you can walk out your door and catch a bus anytime.

Buses run once an hour, starting from both ends of the country. You might have heard stories about the wild bus rides here in Belize; and how buses race each other to pick up passengers along the road. We used to get some pretty exciting rides for our money. But the government put a stop to this by requiring rival bus companies to travel in opposite directions to each other.

Taxi cabs are easy to find and relatively inexpensive, as in most Third World countries. Since the average person cannot afford a car, bus and taxi transportation is the norm. For intermediate distances that are too far to walk, and too short for a bus ride; and for any special occasions, a taxi is used. By our standards they're not expensive, the fare is usually $2.50 per "drop" (ride). And when you consider all the fuel costs and the upkeep of a car. . .well it's hard to decide.

In Belize gasoline costs around $2.35 per gallon. On the

other hand Butane costs $1 per gallon (and only 50¢ in nearby Mexico) so we're starting to see more butane powered vehicles.

Seriously consider bringing a bicycle if you move to Belize. You can buy one here but they are very expensive. Used bikes can cost $100. I've seen some new rugged bikes made in mainland China for around $200.

You can even bring a bike on the plane. You can get a cardboard bicycle box from any bike store and then check it on the airplane with you, just like you would any other piece of luggage. I did.

Most Belizean towns are just the right size to bicycle around in. However, this is not recommended if you're hard of hearing--large sugar cane trucks can roar up behind you before you're aware of it.

All this talk about buses, bikes and taxi cabs is fine you may be thinking to yourself . . . but I love my car! And I can't stand the thought of going anywhere without it. Well, you may want to reconsider once you hear what happens when you get to to Belize.

First of all you're hit with the import duty (72% of *Bluebook* value) before you can permanently bring your car into the country. Here's how it works: If you're entering Belize with a vehicle for the first time and plan to stay less than 3 months, you can get a temporary permit (T.P.). This will allow you to bring your car in without paying the duty.

The T.P. will be issued for 30 days, at the end of that time period, if you want to stay longer, you have to return to the border or go to the Customs Dept. in Belize City and request an extension. Two extensions are the maximum, so at the end of 90 days you either have to pay duty or take your car out of the country

Of course, you can pay the duty the day you enter Belize (use a broker, it's necessary). But if you're not sure you're going to stay, don't. Duty is not refundable. Once you pay duty, you're allowed to sell your car if you want. If you haven't figured it out yet, the reason the government does all of this is to get their cut up front, should you decide to sell your car in Belize.

So if you're just driving down to check out the situation, definitely ask for the T.P., even if you're 99% sure you want to stay sight unseen. Some drive down, sell their car and fly back. You can always get more for your car in Belize, then in the U.S.

Car Tips

Don't ever fix up the outside of a car before you bring it to Belize. The drive down here will ruin any new paint job. And when you go to pay your duty your car will first be "valued." That means that a Customs officer looks over your car and decides how much it's worth. You then have to pay a percentage of that as duty. So the more your car is valued at, the more duty you pay. But the value is determined only by the condition of the body! Not much else is taken into account. So even if your car has no engine; but has a shiny new paint job, it's valued higher than a vehicle in good running condition, but with an ugly body, and of course you'll have to pay more.

If you definitely want to bring a car to Belize, the key is to bring something old and ugly (10 years or more). Make sure it runs good, but looks bad (you can always paint it later).

Because of the rough roads; flat tires can be a daily occurrence, and tires are expensive in Belize. So, if you drive the back roads a lot, buy bias ply tires. They stand up much better then radials do, expect to pay about $80 apiece in Belize. They're available in Belize City at Bandag Tyres, 44 Central American Blvd., Tel. 02-73214.

Belizean mechanics for the most part are honest, do good work, and are inexpensive. We had one make a "house call" on our old clunker; he spent about one hour working on it and the fee was $5 plus parts. So there's a plus for those who want to bring their car.

Car Insurance

You must purchase Belizean insurance before you enter your car in the country. Insurance is available at all borders. You can buy it by the day, week, month quarter, or year. It's cheaper by the year. We pay $130 a year, but carry only the minimum.

Driver's License

Getting a "driving license" as they call it in Belize is easy. You'll need: A) a Xerox copy of your present valid driver's license. (B) Two passport sized photos. (C) $20 and (D) Proof that you're an insured driver.

Here comes the fun part:

1) First go to the local *Department of Transport*, usually located just a stones throw away from the local post office. There you'll meet a "friendly" licensing officer, who will fill out the form for you. Give him your xerox copy and the 2 pictures of yourself.

2) The licensing officer will then send you to the local government health clinic (also nearby) with a medical examination form,. You may go to a private doctor for this exam, if you wish. At the government clinic, tell the Nun on duty why you're there. She'll then show you a small box and tell you that this is a free examination; but before the doctor can see you, they'd appreciate a contribution. She'll come back a little while later and ask if you've made your contribution yet. Then she'll take you in to see a harried government doctor. He will not take time to look up at you. Viewing only your paper work, he'll ask if you've

made your contribution yet. You say yes. He signs your medical form; and you've passed your physical exam.

3) Back at the Department of Transport, they'll give you all your paper work back. Take it to the cashier and pay the fee. Now it gets weird. . .if it's your birthday or within a few days of it, you're OK. . . if not, hold on for some strange logic.

The fee covers you until your next birthday. Say this is August and your birthday falls on November 1st. You will have to renew your license on the 1st of November, just 3 months away! "What happened to my year?" you may ask. Well. . . that was it. They only license from birth date to birth date, regardless of the day you came in to apply. You can buy two years at a time if that makes you feel any better.

4) Come back in a week or two and they'll dig through a pile of licenses until they find the one with your picture on it. Now you're all set to go.

Vehicle Registration

To register your vehicle in Belize, you'll need (A) your current motor vehicle registration card. (B) your title. (C) proof of Belizean auto insurance. (D) the 3 pages from the *Import Entry EX* form that you received when you paid the duty on your car at the border.

The registration fee is $12.50. Tags will cost around $95 a year. This is rated on a sliding scale. depending on the year and make of your vehicle. If you want you can pay this on a yearly, semi-yearly, or even on a quarterly basis.

They may or may not inspect your vehicle. If they do, they'll probably look at your brake lights, tail lights, head lights and turn indicators. They may ask you to sound your horn, operate your wind shield wipers, and test your brakes.

How soon should you register your vehicle after paying the duty? No one knows for sure; everyone we asked gave us a different answer. We suggest that you register your vehicle the day after your 90 day T.P. expires. The same goes for getting your Belizean driving license. Traffic wardens regularly stop traffic and check for these things. You can see why some choose not to have a car because of the added expense and hassle.

Air Taxi

There is also very good air service available, to destinations within Belize. Maya Air and Tropic Air fly from one end of the country to the other, as well as to the cayes. The fares are not too bad. For example from Belize City to San Pedro, Ambergris Caye is $35 one way. You save a few dollars on a round trip ticket.

There are published stops. but the schedules are flexible. If you want to go to some little out of the way place and it's on the way to one of their stops, they'll put you down there since there are make-shift landing strips practically everywhere that's anywhere.

Climate

Mention that you're thinking about going to Belize and those who want to be negative will say something like, "Sure it's pretty there, but it's hot and disgustingly humid all the time. . . uggh"

I've read three different official descriptions of Belize's climate: Tropical, semi-tropical and sub-tropical --pick the one you like. The average year-round temperature is 79 degrees. There are two seasons, wet and dry. Wet season is June to January, in some parts of the country.

Even though the country is only 180 miles long there is a dramatic change in rainfall. At Corozal, in the north, it's 50 inches a year. and at Punta Gorda in the south, it's 160 inches (I've heard as high as 200 inches).

April and May are the dry months.   They're also the hottest months.   June and July are wet and cooler.   In August there's a 2-week period where the breeze stops and it can be unbearably hot and humid. In September though, the rains start again and it's very very warm until November. Then; December, January, and February, have absolutely perfect weather.

How hot is it?   Well, it's a different kind of hot.   The sun is very strong, from about 8 a.m. till around 2:30 p.m. You just don't go out for very long without some kind of protection from the sun, like a straw hat or umbrella. Later in the day, the sun is low enough in the sky that it's quite pleasant to be out.   Even during the hottest time of day, you can step into your house and it's cool.   And I don't mean a hermetically sealed air-conditioned house either.

And as for the humidity, I don't have all the figures on this one, but I'll tell you how it feels, because it's kind of hard to explain.   While, technically, it's humid in Belize, it just doesn't feel humid most of the time because of the trade winds.   It doesn't feel anything like New York in August, or New Orleans in July.

We vacationed in Washington D.C. once in the month of June. I can start to perspire just thinking of that trip.   It's nothing like that in Belize.

I had lived in a semi-arid region of the United States all my life and suffered from what I call "fear-of-humidity." The biggest concern I had about moving to Belize was the climate.   How would I adapt to it?

Bill had spent time in the tropics before and loved it. But I had only visited the tropics once and that was during the dry season.   Now here we were moving everything we owned down to tropical Belize in our RV.

As we made our way through Texas, I was getting a bit nervous. What if we were making a mistake? What if I couldn't handle the tropical climate and we had to turn around and come back?

We reached Brownsville around sundown and the September sky was a brilliant golden blaze. We found the trailer park we were to stay in that evening; our last before crossing the border into Mexico in the morning.

As evening fell, the warm sunny afternoon became a heavy, oppressive, muggy night. I remember walking around the park actually feeling (despite the fact that I was wearing a thin dress and sandals) that I had a wool blanket dipped in steaming hot water on my back. The air was thick and heavy, and it was hard to breathe. At some point, it dawned on me: "This is humidity. . . I don't like it!"

Inside our RV the situation was even worse. We felt like it might take years off our life span to spend much time in there.

As Bill was making final preparations on the RV, I gasped: "It's humid here."

"Yeah, that's Texas all right. Freezes in the winter; hot and muggy in the summer. Lived here for years. . .hated it!"

"But if it's this bad here, how much worse will it be in Belize this time of year?"

"Oh, no, Belize is great. You get the breeze off the Caribbean, It's nothing like this. After a few weeks in the tropics your body adapts and you feel great."

I wandered off in a zombie-like state. It was now 10:30 at night, the trailer park was filled with people walking around and talking. These were people from all over the U.S. and Canada, who come to Brownsville to escape the cold. They call themselves "snowbirds." I couldn't imagine why they'd come to this place, though. The climate there, in my opinion, was not enjoyable. It was like a form of punishment.

Somehow, I got involved in a conversation with a woman who lived there "full-time."
"Where you headed?" she asked.
"Belize" I replied.
"Why?" she asked.
"We're moving there."
"Where are you from?" she asked.
"California."
"California! You're moving from California to Belize? It's hot and humid--and they have bugs!"
As she said this, I realized that now that I was standing still, the sweat that was running down my legs was actually forming pools, and small rivulets could begin at any time to flow through the dirt streets of the trailer park. I noticed that, because during our conversation, I had to repeatedly bend down to swat giant Texas sized mosquitoes from my ankles.

As soon as we got out of Texas, that terrible heat and humidity was gone and we've never experienced it since then. At first, it did seem hot in Belize (but not that hot). But, we got used to it. And now we love the tropical weather.

We helped our bodies adapt by drinking lots of water, wearing all cotton clothes and taking it easy during the hot part of the day. That's when you get in your hammock time!

In fact, we've gotten so used to that lovely tropical heat, that anything less seems cold. Occasionally in Belize, we get "Northers," cold fronts that move in very rapidly. One morning, we woke up to find the warm trade winds had turned chilly. As we dug out some winter clothes, we tried to guess what the temperature was.
"It was about 86 yesterday, but it must be in the fifties right now." I called out, as I slipped into a full set of thermal underwear; blue jeans, ski sweater, hat, and completed my ensemble with a scarf.
Bill wore a coat inside the house most of the day, and

claimed it was in the forties.

"How could the temperature drop so quickly," we wondered. Finally, I remembered a little thermometer out on the veranda. I couldn't believe my eyes when I read it. It said: 72°F.

So, you see, not only do you get used to the tropical heat, but anything less is uncomfortable.

We're not saying the weather in Belize is perfect, we're just saying we like it; and so do a lot of other Gringos. Maybe you will too.

Different climates appeal to different people, Some people live in Alaska, for example, and love it. We've spent time in Alaska and even though we enjoyed it's great natural beauty, we consider it a kind of Arctic torture chamber.

Another thing to remember in Belize is: Even though it may get warmer than you'd like; there's never any bone-chilling cold weather, never any freezing rain, hail, or snow; and never any icy roads to walk or drive on. You'll never have icy-cold fingers, toes, ears, or noses; and never any struggling to get out of a warm bed on a frosty morning.

Early morning coffee overlooking the Caribbean

Chapter 9
Red Tape

There's plenty of it in Belize. For such a small country with such a small population it seems to have more than its share of red tape.

You will be concerned primarily with immigration red tape. You need a passport to enter Belize. No visa is required for citizens of the United States, Canada and the U.K. Citizens of other countries should inquire of the Belizean Consulate.

The government of Belize has never really encouraged tourism in the true sense of the word, or made it easy to come to visit or to live in Belize. Belize has not been as hospitable, shall we say, to visitors as Mexico has. It is easier now than it was years ago. Back then we heard stories of people being turned away because they had long hair or a back-pack, but that all changed with Ecotourism. Officially you're supposed to have $50 per person per day for the duration of your visit. We know for a fact, this is not enforced.

However, at the border they may ask you how much cash you have. You can tell them: "I have "X" amount of dollars in cash as well as travelers checks and credit cards." As long as your appearance isn't sloppy, there shouldn't be a problem.

A free visitors permit will be stamped into your passport

when you cross the border into Belize. Permits are only issued for 30 days. If you wish to stay longer; you'll have to return to the border, exit the country, and then return later. You will be allowed to re-enter the same day. You can do this indefinitely. We know some who have done it for years. You can also go to Immigration in Belize City or Belmopan and get a 30 day extension on your Visitors permit for the cost of $12.50 US per person.

The Immigration Department would like you to buy six months at a time. They'll be glad to "sell" you a semiannual stay, at $12.50 per month times 6 months. This eliminates the need to exit the country every month or travel to Belize City or Belmopan.

What if you decide to retire in Belize and don't want to be bothered with immigration every 30 days or 6 months. As a retiree you have a real advantage. You can obtain permanent residency very easily. You can then live here for as long as you like, with all the rights of a Belizean citizen, (except voting and serving in the armed forces) but without giving up your U.S. or Canadian citizenship. As a retired resident you qualify for "free" government land and are not required to pay income tax on any money earned or received from outside the country. (See Special Report: *Buying Property/Building a House in Belize*)

The usual procedure for obtaining residency is to first go to Belmopan and pick up the official residency forms. You can save yourself a long trip to Belmopan by buying the forms from Angelus Press at #10 Queen St. Belize City, Tel. 02-35777.

Complete these forms and take them to Belmopan Immigration. (About a 1 hour bus ride from Belize City). To Apply you must have: (1) proof of your income (Social Security, pension, etc.) (2) a letter from your bank in the U.S. or Canada showing your account number and balance (there is no minimum amount required for retirees) (3) the completed medical form and chest X-rays (4) a police

clearance letter from home (5) three passport type photos.
A $300 deposit is payable at the time you turn in your application. Only the head of the family has to pay the deposit. The deposit is returned to you after you have lived in Belize for 3 years. If you have a Belizean friend sponsor you, the three hundred dollar fee can be waived. (See our Special Report: *How to Become a Resident of Belize*).

For items #1 and #2: You will have to bring proof of income and a bank statement from back home with you.

For Item #3: The form now stipulates that your medical exam and lab work be done in Belize. We recommend you go to a private doctor for this; it will be much quicker and easier than dealing with the government clinic. The doctor will charge from $10 - $20, and the lab work, a VDRL and HIV test, will run another $35. You can have all of this done in one day. When we had ours done in the U.S. it cost us $275 each, and we had to wait weeks for the results.

For item #4: The police letter: This can be obtained by contacting the police department in the city where you now live. Tell them you need a clearance letter it'll cost around $10 in most cities. In Belize it's called a *Police Certificate of Character*. Your local police will fingerprint you and run a record check, then "hopefully" issue a letter stating you have not been involved in any criminal activity. This takes at least one week.

It's a good idea to bring this with you, even if you're not sure you want to stay in Belize, Because you can't apply for residency without it. (To get a police letter in Belize, see our special Report)

After all of this there's an additional $100 non-refundable processing fee the day your paper work is approved (Immigration will not mention this beforehand).

How long will it take to get residency? Nobody knows.

But probably not more than 3 to 6 months from the day you turn in your papers (for a retiree). A friend of ours who has an Army pension, Social Security and a retirement plan from his last employer, got his residency in one day! Now that's a record. It had to be a fluke! Don't expect anything like that to happen to you. (If you're not retired and are still of working age this can be a hard nut to crack. But it can be done--you can get your residency with some hard work. Again, we say see our Special Report).

A recently enacted Immigration law aimed at discouraging Central Americans from immigrating to Belize, requires a 1 year waiting period before applying for Permanent Residency. **This law does not apply to retirees.** But, if told it does; tactfully ask the officer to look it up for you. (Immigration: Tel. 08-22611, 08-22423, Fax 08-22662).

Be sure to check back in a few weeks after submitting your application and see if your residency has been approved. Please don't get upset when they tell you they've lost your paper work and that you'll have to apply all over again. This is all very normal. Politely ask them to look again and in a little while they'll find it.

By obtaining permanent resident status, as a "retiree" you're promising the government of Belize that you will not do any work for which you'll get paid, from Belizean sources. You can still work, but the money earned must come from outside Belize. Say you're an artist, photographer or writer. You can work at your craft day and night in Belize, as long as your work is sold outside Belize.

Until your residency is approved you'll have to continue getting your 30 day extensions. This isn't as bad as it sounds. Just plan to go over to Chetumal, Mexico or Melchor del Mencos, Guatemala to shop once a month and they'll automatically extend you 30 days each time, usually with no questions asked. If they do ask why you've been in Belize so long, tell them you've applied for residency and your papers are processing. That will satisfy them.

Chapter 10
Moving to Belize

The big decision you'll have to make is whether to haul it, ship it, or buy it? You can either bring your household items from home or buy what you need, once you get to Belize. Both ways have their advantages and disadvantages.

Certain things, like furniture and beds for example, are not difficult to find in Belize. Since such items are usually of excellent quality and can be purchased at a reasonable price, there's no real reason to drag yours down with you.

Other things, however, (generally anything with a plug) will be very expensive if you decide to buy it new in Belize. Things we take for granted at home can be prohibitively expensive in Belize.

So what do you do? Many, (after they're sure they want to move to Belize) load such appliances as refrigerator, washing machine, dryer, etc. on either a truck or a trailer and drive them down. But, since the Mexican government instituted their "Transmigrado" (Transmigration Fee) around 1991 this is harder to do and can be quite costly. Here's how it works: Any vehicle hauling "freight" thru Mexico to Central or South America must post a "bond" upon entering Mexico. This is to insure Mexico that should the driver illegally sell his freight in Mexico, they'll get their cut (duty) first. The problem is your household items may be considered "freight" by the Mexican authorities and require a bond. This cost about $600 plus $100 for a broker, at each end to do and undo. They may also require a guard to ride all the way thru Mexico with you, to make sure you don't sell your stuff.

The key here is to get into Mexico as a tourist and avoid the transmigration fee altogether. There are a number of things you can do: (1) As we mentioned earlier, don't even tell the Mexicans your ultimate destination is Belize. When they ask you where you're going, tell them where you'll be staying in Mexico. (2) Don't pull a trailer. It's pretty hard to convince someone you're on a sight seeing trip when you're dragging a double capacity washer, dryer and refrigerator around with you. Pack your household things into a car or van. Pack them discreetly into plastic storage bins. Take anything new out of its box or package. The more used it looks the better. We're talking about appliances, electronic gadgetry, and gizmos; not clothes, books, etc. You won't have any problems with these.

Once you have permanent residency status in Belize, you can bring virtually all your household belongings into the country with out paying duty; excluding your vehicle. But if you bring things in before this, you'll probably have to pay duty when you enter the country. We say "probably" because sometimes they'll let you through without paying. How much you pay depends on the day, time, and the mood of the Customs Officer on duty.

It's usually better to cross the border in the evening, any time after 5 p.m. The night shift is not as frazzled as the day shift, and are usually in a better mood (unless it happens to be a holiday, and they're working, then nobody is happy). The rules are very flexible, and it's up to the discretion of the Customs Officer how much duty to charge you.

Bringing furniture in requires an importation permit. This is because furniture is produced in Belize; the permit is free--getting it--is the problem. This held a friend of ours up at the border for 3 days! He was finally able to bring everything in, but what a headache! I wondered if it was really worth all the hassle when I saw the timeworn furniture our friends had just dragged three thousand miles. His wife said she was very attached to her family "heirlooms" and wouldn't live in Belize without them.

If you should get held up at the border don't panic. It's usually over some little form they don't have on hand. (For example, they never ever have any of the furniture importation forms available). And you'll have to go to Belize City or Belmopan to get it. Such is life in a country with so few Xerox machines.

Border problems are usually with Customs and not Immigration, so even if they won't let your things in, they will usually let you in.   So just leave your things at the border (they'll be safe). This includes vehicles, boats, trailers --big things.

Go to Corozal, check into a hotel, and cool off. This is nothing to get upset about.   Next day; go back to the border and try again. If it's a weekend, you may have to wait until Monday when all the Customs personnel who do processing are there.

Don't worry, you'll get all your things in eventually. Sometimes if you leave and come back after the shift change it will make a big difference.

We met a resourceful fellow who was having major problems getting his large inflatable boat into Belize. He left it at the border for several days. Finally in disgust, he exited Belize taking his boat with him. He spent the night in Mexico and returned the very next day. He had taken the time to deflate his boat and fold it up into a neat little square that now sat in the corner of his pickup bed. The same customs officers were on duty! --he had no problems.

What ever you do, don't make the mistake of flying off the handle at the border officers. That will only make matters worse. And don't offer a "tip" in advance either, that won't work here. These guys don't want money, they want respect. Act almost reverential, if you have to. They want to feel that they're in control. Play the game. Do whatever they ask, no matter how small and inconsequential it may seem to you.

But, say you feel you're not being treated fairly; maybe you think they're trying to charge you too much import duty; then try bargaining with them. Show them the defects in your vehicle, boat, etc. If you tell them how little cash you have on hand, they will sometimes lower the duty.

Or, you can request that they impound your property to Belize City. We have friends who do this regularly, because they feel that the customs people in Belize City go strictly by the book, giving them a better deal.

We heard about a fellow who got to the border with his truck full of stuff on a Friday night. He could get in, but his truck couldn't. (Customs only processes vehicles 8:00 am to 2:30 p.m. Monday thru Friday). He had to be in Belize City on Saturday morning to attend a conference. He knew he could enter the country with a Customs guard, so he wasn't worried. He showed up at the conference with the bored guard glued to his side. With only slight embarrassment, he explained how he came to have such a strange escort.

Now that you've heard about some of the problems with bringing your household items into the country by yourself, you might want to consider other options.

One is renting a furnished house. We've seen houses for rent with everything including the kitchen utensils They're not common, but they do exist.

Or you might sell your household things in the U.S. and use the money to buy all new furniture and household items that are made locally.

If you can't bear the idea of parting with your family "heirlooms" you could have them shipped. There are a few companies that ship from Houston Texas or from Florida right to Belize City.

Hyde Shipping sails from Port Everglades every Friday and arrives in Belize City on Monday. For rates and bookings contact: Hyde Shipping, 10025 N.W. 116th Way, Suite 1, Medley, FL 33178, Tel. 1-800-323-3906, Fax 305-913-4900.

Tropical Shipping sails from Port Everglades every Thursday and arrives in Belize City on Monday. Contact: Tropical Shipping, 12501 N.W. 38 Ave., Opa Loca, FL 33054, Tel. 1-800-367-6200, Fax 305-953-4551.

Keep in mind that your lifestyle is going to be different in Belize, you may not need all the things that you thought you could never live without.   After all Belizeans live without them.

For example a washing machine--which most Americans consider as necessary to life as oxygen--is seldom seen in Belize and laundromats do not exist per se. Women wash by hand on scrub boards and hang their clothes in the sun to dry. (The clothes come out spotless) Some Americans have found that it's not that bad washing by hand. Others pay wash women to do it for them. It's very cheap, but hard on your clothes. So you see, life without a washing machine is possible. Your personal situation will dictate what's best for you. What about us?. . . we use a washing machine; and also a local lady who washes and irons for us. We pay about $7.50 a day.

If you're an RV'er and travel thousands of mile a year just for the fun of it, a trip to Belize bringing a few household items wouldn't be a big deal to you.

On the other hand an plane ticket might make more sense for you. Even if you fly, you can still bring household stuff with you. A blender could fit in your carry on bag; a hair dryer in your purse. We're experts at this kind of thing now, and could probably get an entire kitchen in a full sized suit case.

Just be sure to take everything apart and pack it well. using a lot of padding (clothes are good for this). Be sure and let the airport people know what you've packed. We had a Mexicana ticket agent nearly run for cover once, when he X-rayed an electric drill in one of our carry on bags.

Seriously though, we'll give you the low down on appliances in Belize:

Stoves are no problem now. You can get good ones in Belize and at reasonable prices. Not like the old days, when we went through all the trouble of finding a small gas range, and then converting it to butane. We dragged the thing 2,500 miles to Belize, only to find much nicer ones on sale everywhere. (All stoves in Belize are either butane, or kerosene, there is no natural gas and we've never seen an electric stove, here).

Refrigerators are a bit more expensive than in the U.S. But you can now bring refrigerators into Belize duty free. So you could go over to Chetumal, Mexico; buy lots of devaluated Pesos with your American dollars and get a nice refrigerator for about what it would cost you in the U.S.

Dishwashers are virtually unheard of in Belize. Toaster ovens and microwaves are available, but very expensive. Bring a small one with you in your carry on luggage...Don't laugh! we've done it more than once.

Vacuum cleaners are available only at "ritzy" appliance stores in Belize City...and they're very expensive. You may get along just fine without one--houses in Belize don't usually have carpets, tiled floors are the norm.

We lived without a vacuum for a couple of years. Eventually, we brought one down--in a piece of hard-sided luggage.   Vacuums are really helpful to have for things other than floors, like bookcases and window sills. (Things can get dusty in Belize during dry season)

Washing machines: This is a hard one, You can buy an American made washing machine (What Belizeans call an "automatic") at Brodies, in Belize City.   The price is high, about half again the price of the same machine in the U.S.

You can buy a cheaper type of washing machine common in Third World countries, called the "Hoover." It's a small portable unit, but it's not automatic.

Some of these units will wash clothes (agitate in soapy water) but will not rinse them.   You have to take your clothes out of the machine and do the rinsing by hand, in a wash tub. Others will rinse the clothes, but don't spin, so you have to wring them out by hand. As inconvenient as they might be--they sure beat the Belizean scrub board.

Renting a House

This could be very difficult, if you didn't have our "sage" advice.   There are no rental offices, no apartment finding services, or rental lists to use. You won't even find signs on most houses that are for rent. So how do you find a house for rent? You've got to be a real self starter in this area.

Now, you have to do something you may not be used to. You'll have to go up to people you don't know and start talking to them. You can start with other North Americans you see in Belize. That won't be so hard. There's a kind of bond that exists among North Americans in foreign countries. People you'd never even speak to back home are instantly your bosom buddies. They'll almost always be glad to help you. You can also ask Belizeans to help you find a house to rent. A lot of Belizeans move to the States. It's estimated that one half of the total population of Belize lives in the U.S. So there are houses left empty. You would never be able to find these on your own, however.

Be out-going and friendly, Talk to people, let them know you're looking for a place to rent. Tell everyone--the taxi driver, the hotel clerk, the shop keeper. Soon you'll have your pick of places. People will start coming to you with stories about their aunt's house by the sea that's been vacant for 2 years, since she moved to Miami. More than likely in a few days you'll have a house to rent.

Another way to find a house to rent is (don't laugh) drive or walk around the area you would like to live in. Look for empty houses. A missing electric meter is a tell-tale sign, as is an "unchopped" (overgrown) yard.

Start asking neighbors about the house. You will eventually find out the whole story. A lot of houses aren't exactly being offered for rent, but the owner wouldn't mind the money coming in. Some friends of ours who live in Cayo rent a beautiful house. One day while sightseeing we passed what could only be described politely as a shack. We couldn't believe it when our friends said this was their landlord's other home. He didn't mind living in a shack, and renting out his beautiful home for extra income.

Remember this: No matter how you find the house, if at all possible have a Belizean approach the owner and ask what the price is. They'll get the real price. If you ask, you may get an inflated price. (There are tourists who will pay this price, at the drop of a hat). However, once they quote the real price, they won't raise it, even after they find out you're an American.

Once we had an older Belizean man who used to sell us fruit negotiate a house for us. He never once told the owner that we were American, until the deal was closed. We saved $100 a month. That was the difference between the tourist price and the Belizean price!

Another way we get a lower rent is by offering to pay several months at a time. If they are asking $125 offer $100 to be paid three months at a time. After you explain your proposal tell them "I will give you $600 BZ ($300 U.S.) right now." and be prepared to back it up with the cash. In the long run you can save money, but if all you have is a small monthly check coming in, this may not be practical

What are the rents like in Belize? Here are some specific examples to give you an idea. We know a couple who rented a very large 3 bedroom house right on the water for $150. It had been rented previously to an American man who paid $250 a month, but they got it in the off season-- a Belizean negotiated the deal for them.

There is a retired couple near us who rent a very nice 3 bedroom house with a hot water heater (rare in Belize) and a detached wash room/work shop. The fenced in yard has fruit trees and is so large it's like a small park. They pay $125. These example are both pretty "luxurious" by Belizean standards, remember Belize is what we would call rustic. You could certainly live well in a smaller and less fancy place. There are some cute little houses, some two bedroom, some three, with nice sized kitchens and bathrooms that rent for around $75 a month. These are very basic.

I've see houses renting for as low as $25 a month! I mean a real house with running water, electricity, a kitchen and an indoor bathroom (although it did need some fixing up). You should be able to rent a place for anywhere between $75 to $200 a month depending on what you want or can afford. Keep in mind that almost any place you move into will probably need a coat of paint. It's just not the custom here to paint a house regularly.

Some of the highest rents in the country are to be found in Belize City. Can you figure that? Expect to pay double or triple or more here, than what you'd pay anywhere else in the country.

Utilities

After you rent a house you'll go to the nearest Belize Electricity Limited office (BEL) and request service locally. This is called getting "current," not to be confused with bringing yourself up to date.

Current is supplied at 110 Volts a.c. There will be a $25 deposit required. This is refundable if you discontinue service. Try to go to the BEL office as soon as possible because they can be very slow in providing service.

Electricity is very expensive in Belize, about 3 times what it costs in the U.S. and the more you use the more it costs per kilowatt hour.

We use electric fans, a microwave, washing machine, lights and a lot of electrical doodads, and we pay between $25 to $40 per month.

Next, stop by the Belize Water and Sewerage office for your "pipe water." This will also take a couple of days to get hooked up. Our water bill is around $20 a month—we use a lot of water. Many Belizeans tell me their water bill is only $3.50 a month because they use rain water from their vat for cooking, drinking, and bathing.

Getting a telephone is not as hard as it used to be. It all

depends on the area that you live in. If you live in an area
that already has phone lines, it shouldn't be too long--
unless they run out of phones again, like they did one year.
(phone sets are provided by the phone company as part of
their service.) You can bring your own handset down with
you.

Telephone service isn't cheap in Belize.   It's $45 for
installation and the monthly bill can be big if you call the
States a lot. You are billed by the unit (8 seconds) for calls
within Belize. Calls to the U.S. and Canada are $1.60 per
minute. Economy time is 10:00 p.m. to 6:00 a.m., at $1
per minute. (This applies only to calls to the U.S.)

Deposit: We're starting to feel downright embarrassed
by how many Americans come down here to Belize and
"forget" to pay their phone bill when they leave. Because of
this the phone company now requires that all foreigners pay
a special deposit of $200 which is refundable when you
discontinue phone service. You can avoid having to pay the
deposit by not having International Direct Dial (IDD) service
on your phone line.   In other words, you can't call outside
Belize; which isn't that bad since you can go to the BTL
office (Belize Telecommunications Limited) and use the
phone there; 8:00 a.m. to 4:30 p.m. Monday thru Friday,
and 8 to 12 on Saturdays. It's not really that inconvenient
for making occasional calls home.

Buying Property

Ever thought of owning your own piece of land?
Growing your own food? Or having the pleasure of building
the house of your dreams?   Some North Americans who
couldn't afford to do this up north, have been able to do
this in Belize; but not without encountering some pitfalls
along the way.

I couldn't begin to give you all the information you need
to have in such limited space. But here's some advice:
BE CAREFUL!

As a foreigner you can buy land in Belize, many do, but there are some risks. We've heard so many "land-deals-gone-bad" stories that we've lost count; even from Belizeans who have been ripped off by other Belizeans

A common ploy is to sell the same piece of land to several people.   Always be sure that the person who is selling you the property actually owns it themselves. They may only lease it from the government, in which case you can go and buy it from the government yourself for a fraction of the price.

If more than one person's name is on the title, make sure that both of them want to sell.

Lee, a friend from California, bought a very nice lot in Corozal Town from a husband and wife (or so he thought). He cleared the land and brought a truck full of building materials down from the U.S. Later he found out that the man was in the process of getting a divorce. The man's wife did not want to sell the land. The bank could not legally give him clear title to the property and in the meantime the man had spent all of Lee's money.

In Belize that's not too much you can do in a case like this. And don't assume that the husband and wife selling you their property are literally each others husband and wife. The term "wife" is not always used in the strict legal sense.

Also, make sure the sellers have paid their back taxes or you'll have to pay them, as the new legal owner.

Make sure that you receive recent survey papers, or you'll be paying for a survey after the sale too.

After checking all of this out with the Lands Department, go to a barrister (lawyer) and have him register it for you. Or you can do it yourself if you know what you're doing. (For more information see our special report: *Buying*

Property/Building a House in Belize)

Jim, a friend of ours, once bought 5 acres of land right outside Punta Gorda. It was a great deal! He only paid $500 and the land was already "chopped" (cleared).

He started to build a beautiful home on the site when the rains came. And much to his chagrin, he found that during the wet season his property was actually waterfront property--two feet under water.

Yet another friend bought three connecting lots on the island of Ambergris Caye. He chopped, and cleared the land; dug a boat slip, and used the dirt from the slip to fill in the low places on his other two lots.

After doing all this work, and finally getting ready to build his dream house, he found that two other Americans had bought this same piece of land from the previous owner.

As it turned out he can legally keep the land because he cleared it--that means a lot to the Belizean Government. But the other two Americans were out the money they'd paid.

Are these stories starting to sound like swampland tales from Florida? This calls to mind another tip: Physically get out and walk around on a piece of land before you buy it. We looked at a beautiful lot that had just been sold to some rich Americans. It was right on the lagoon in San Pedro, Ambergris Caye. There was rich, lush foliage growing profusely on the lot. The only problem is that there's no lot there! It's really just a bunch of red mangrove trees growing in about six inches of water.

With all this in mind, we can say that there are still some great real estate deals in Belize. By our standards, the land is dirt cheap. Please help keep it that way.

The Belizean government has enacted laws to prevent foreigners from speculating with land. But in spite of this we have seen ocean front lots change hands three or four times and double or triple in price each time. All this in just a few months after being placed on the market.

One day we were looking at some beautiful ocean front property offered by a developer in Placencia. We noticed that they were laid out next to some government lots. The beach-front lots the developer offered had an astronomical price tag; but the government lots were being offered free to Belizeans without land.

But guess what? As a resident you could qualify for one small lot in town and 10 acres outside city limits. (See our report)

Building a House

After hearing all theses horror stories do you still want to build the house of your dreams? A lot of people see land going at "dirt cheap" prices and their heads start spinning. Before you know it they are building their own Hearst Castle.

Admittedly labor costs are a fraction of what they are in the U.S.; but don't be fooled by the "cheap" labor (around $25 a day). It might take twice as long to build your dream house--or longer.

You have to be willing to stay at the work site everyday. We're not saying you won't get an honest day's work out of your crew, but you have to be there physically to get the job done right--even with a contractor. And any time you leave the job site there's a good chance your crew will take an extended break.

Beach front property Placencia

Caye Chapel

Chapter 11
Places to Go, Things to Do

There's lots to see in beautiful Belize, here is but a sampling.

Jaguar Preserve

Belize has the world's first and only. It is located south of Dangriga at Maya Center. (Mile 14 on the Southern Highway). From there go west 7 miles. Cabins are available and camping is permitted. But there's no food available, bring your own.

This is a wildlife sanctuary within a forest reserve, so even if you don't get to see a jaguar, you can still enjoy the nature trails. Since it rains here from June through January, you should inquire about conditions and facilities at the Audubon Society, #12 Fort Street, Belize City, telephone 02-34988 or inquire at the Pelican Beach resort in Dangriga.

Mountain Pine Ridge

This is a 300-square-mile forest reserve, that is home to some fantastic scenery. Here on the west slope of the Maya Mountains, waterfalls tumble down 1,600 feet to river valleys thick with hardwood forest and orchids.

It's located on the Western Highway. Georgeville is the junction for the road that takes you to Mountain Pine Ridge.

It can be explored by vehicle, on foot, mountain bike, or horseback.   You need a pretty rugged vehicle to make the trip.

The Belize Zoo

It's been said that it isn't really a zoo, it is just a cleared spot in the jungle, with some wire mesh enclosures to separate you from the animals.   We think it's great, and highly recommend you stop in.

The keel-billed toucan who lives in the mango tree out in the open yard is very friendly.   The first time I saw the colors on his bill it brought tears to my eyes. (They were so brilliant and beautiful, they looked as if they had come off the palette of a grand artist). The sleek, majestic jaguar was also breathtaking.

While the Belize Zoo doesn't have a snack bar, or a fancy gift shop, it does have a fascinating collection of rare and interesting wildlife.   Don't miss it.

You can get there by catching any Belize City to San Ignacio bus.   Ask the driver to drop you off at the zoo. You can walk in the rest of the way from the main road.

The zoo is at mile 28.8 on the Western Highway.   It is open 10 a.m. to 4:30 p.m. everyday.   Admission is $5.

The Baboon Sanctuary
The first thing you should know is that there are no baboons in Belize.   At least what we think of as baboons. The black howler monkey thrives here, and in Creole they're called "baboons."

This sanctuary consists of privately owned lands.   The owners have joined together to preserve food trees and vegetation along the Belize River, necessary to black howler life.   This area is also home to about 200 species of birds as well as other wildlife.

Contact the Audubon Society in Belize City before you visit. A guide is required and a guide book is available. You can take a boat, or walk on trails and see groups of howlers swinging through the trees. Once you hear their ear-splitting call you'll understand how they got their name.

Boat Races

The Baron Bliss Annual Yacht Regatta, held in Belize City every March 9th.

The Annual Elma B. Anniversary Boat Race, held at Gale's Point on July 12th.

The Sarteneja Easter Sunday regatta, in Sarteneja, Corozal District.

Hol Chan Marine Reserve

Some of the worlds best diving about 4 miles southeast of San Pedro Ambergris Caye. This is a 5-square mile reserve teaming with more than 500 species of fish.

Blue Hole
(At Lighthouse Reef)

Maybe you saw this famous Belizean diving spot on the Jacques Cousteau special a few years back. The Blue Hole is a nearly perfect hole 300 feet across and 400 feet deep. Scientist theorize it was made by the collapse of an underwater cavern, creating a giant underwater sinkhole, filled with dramatic stalagmite and stalactite formations.

Crooked Tree Wildlife Sanctuary

Crooked Tree is a the foremost bird sanctuary in Central America. Look for the sign about 20 minutes south of Orange Walk, located on an island at the end of a 3½ mile long causeway. A real must for birders.

Golf

Orange Walk has the oldest and only golf course in Belize.   Built for the British employees of Belize Sugar Industries Ltd.   It's a private course open to employees of BSI and a few of the remaining members of British Forces Belize.

There is much much more to see and do than we can include in this book, some things you'll have to see for yourself.

Is Belize for you?

Only you can decide if Belize is for you. We strongly encourage you to visit before you decide to make a permanent move. We know some of you are saying "I can't afford it, I'll just move down." But please don't burn your bridges behind you.   Wait until you know what you're getting into. Consider a six month trial move. We love Belize, but we're not sure if you will.

Our best advice is: If you're an aging Indiana Jones, go for it! If you're not, still go for it, but go more slowly.

Appendix

Useful Items

Here are a few things we would not go to Belize without:

Mosquito net:

Straw hat: Don't count on buying one in Belize... Mexico or Guatemala maybe.

Very dark Sunglasses: The glare, especially on the cayes can be a killer.

Bug repellent: Anything with DET is effective, although toxic. We use "Off!" I like an aerosol so I can spray a fine mist over my legs and feet without contaminating my hands.

Cotton clothes: including underwear.

Walking shoes: Get something that has a sole with a good grip.

Umbrella: Preferably not a black one. (I have a theory about solar heating).

Solar shower: If you want a hot shower in Belize, you'll have to bring your own. You can get this at a camping store. It is a plastic bag, black on one side with a plastic nozzle. In a few hours you'll have a shower hotter than you can stand. Once you're settled you can get something more permanent like an electric, on–demand, hot water shower head. They're available in Belize, and costs about $40, they look and sound dangerous, but work great!

Plastic water bottle: The kind bicyclists use is good. They're available in sporting goods stores. We always carry water with us in Belize.

Sunscreen: Never underestimate the power of the tropical sun.   Thirty minutes can leave you fried.

Toilet Paper: Carry it with you at all times while traveling. You won't regret it.

Small pocket calculator: Handy when exchanging foreign currencies.

Toilet paper can be a luxury item when traveling the Third World.

Public and Bank Holidays

New Year's day	January 1
Barron Bliss Day	March 9
Good Friday	
Holy Saturday	
Easter Monday	
Labour Day	May 1
Commonwealth Day	May 24
St. George's Caye Day	September 10
Independence Day	September 21
Columbus Day	October 12
Garifuna Settlement Day	November 19
Christmas Day	December 25
Boxing Day	December 26

Don't expect to find any stores or businesses open on these days; everything is closed!

Belize City from the Swing Bridge

Resources

Recommended Reading

Many of these can be found in your local library or book store. To order from Preview Publishing, use the order blank at the back of the book.

Periodicals on Belize

Bill & Claire Gray's Belize Retirement Newsletter
Keep up-to-date on what's happening in Belize. Published quarterly in Belize. One year air-mail subscription $35.

Belize First - Your Guide to Travel and Life in Belize
The best magazine on Belize we've seen. Packed with information, each issue is like a mini-book. From Equator Travel Publications, Candler, North Carolina. One year subscription, 5 issues $29.

Special Reports by Bill & Claire Gray

How to Become a Resident of Belize
The ins and outs of immigration and legal requirements. How to avoid the time consuming paper chase. Where to go, what to do, and what to say. Contains all the necessary government forms. ISBN 1-880862-01-8   27 pages $19.95

Starting a Business/Working in Belize
Shows you in detail how to take advantage of this entrepreneur's paradise. What licenses you need and don't

need. How to get a work permit. What wages to pay. How to qualify for a 20 year tax holiday.
ISBN 1-880862-00-X   36 pages $19.95

Gringo Gardening...How to Garden in Belize --Grow Food in the Tropics Where, when, and what to plant. How to control pests and other critters. Illustrated.
ISBN 1-880862-02-6   25 pages $16.95

Cooking and Eating in Belize
Shows you how to enjoy new and deliciously different Belizean dishes. How to prepare your old favorites from foods found in Belizean markets. Loaded with recipes for Belizean delicacies and American dishes adapted to the Belizean kitchen.
ISBN 1-880862-03-4   28 pages $16.95

Buying Property/Building a House in Belize
As a foreigner, not only can you own land in Belize, you can even get land practically free from the Belizean Government! Find out how, along with advice on the best types of houses to build. Complete listings of building material suppliers, contractors, and real-estate agents in Belize.
ISBN 1-88062-04-2   56 Pages $19.95

Belize Resource Directory
Updated yearly. Listings from A to Z of everyplace and everything you'll need in Belize.   Names, addresses, telephone, and fax numbers for Belizean government offices and services, (including immigration and customs) airlines serving Belize, air cargo services, building material suppliers, shipping companies. Includes a town by town, district by district section with listings for Police, and Fire Departments, hospitals, telephone office, electricity office. water dept., banks. Use it here while planning your trip/move to Belize, use it there to cut through the hassles.
ISBN 1-880862-05-0   112 Pages $24.95

Bill and Claire's Hotel & Restaurant Guide to Belize
A country wide guide of where to stay and where to eat.
Names, addresses, telephone and fax numbers. All price
ranges ISBN 1-88062-07-7 30 pages $19.95

These reports are available only through Preview Publishing,
see the order blank on the last page of this book.

Belize Retirement Guide
You can Live in a Tropical Paradise on $450 a Month!

Bill & Claire Gray
4th Edition

· The only book of its kind anywhere!

Learn how you can enjoy: Warm, sunny
weather year round · Fresh seafood
· Luscious tropical fruits · Some of
the best fishing, diving, and boating on
the second longest barrier reef on earth
· And do it all while living on your
social security check alone
· Find out about Belize, the English speaking tropical
paradise you can drive to · 124 pages · Photos

$29.95

Belize: Adventures in Nature
By Steel Wotkyns and Richard Mahler
Guides you through all the natural wonders of Belize, with
emphasis on wildlife and conservation efforts. Contains
color photographs of Belize. Detailed information on the
Belize Zoo and Tropical Education Center, Baboon
Sanctuary, The Jaguar Preserve and much more. 408 pages
$18.95

Belize Guide
By Paul Glassman
The first guide book written on Belize, now in its 5th edition. Interesting historical information, as well as specific places to stay and eat. Locations and details an many of the ruins and archaeological sites in Belize. 281 pages $14.95

Guide to Belize
Bradt Publishing in the U.K. is known for their great travel guides, their latest is on Belize. 200 pages $15.95

Adventure Guide to Belize
By Harry Pariser. Maps, color photos, all types of accommodations. from camping to luxury resorts. 288 pages $14.95

The New Key to Belize
By Stacy Ritz. A comprehensive guide book with emphasis on enjoying the natural wonders of Belize. Details on food and lodging; color photos, drawings. 228 pages $14.95

Belize Handbook
by Chicki Mallan
A comprehensive travel guide book on Belize. Detailed lists of where to stay and eat while in Belize, with telephone and fax numbers. Worth its weight in gold if you are planning a visit to Belize. Lots of photos, both black and white plus color. 263 pages $14.95

Cruising Guide to Belize and Mexico's Caribbean Coast
By Freya Rauscher. Includes Guatemala's Rio Dulce. Pilotage, weather, customs, chartering. This is a large sized volume with complete charts locating all points of interest afloat and ashore. 288 photo filled pages. Pullout charts. $34.95

Travelers Reference Map of Belize
2nd edition. Large fold-out 21" X 34" full color map. Topographical shading. Points of interest. $12.95

Road Map of Belize
Incredibly detailed road map of the entire country of Belize with street map of Belize City on the other side. Fully indexed. $7.95

Map of Ambergris Caye Belize
Includes adjacent cayes and inset map of San Pedro $10.95

Map of Central America
Belize, Guatemala, Honduras, El Salvador, Nicaragua, Costa Rica, Panama. $10.95

Parrots Wood
By Erma Fisk. The true story of an 80 year old American woman who came to stay in Belize and study tropical birds. 240 pages $14.95

Belize Telephone Directory
Entire country covered. Telephone, fax numbers and addresses for residential, business and government $25

Books by Emory King

American Emory King was shipwrecked in Belize in 1953 and has been there ever since. He has become the unofficial historian and resident authority on Belize. Until now his books have only been available in Belize.

Emory King's Drivers Guide to Beautiful Belize
(Up-dated yearly) Mile by mile guide to touring Belize by car. 56 pages. $12

How to Invest, Visit or Retire in Belize
Over 40 years of living in Belize has made him an expert. 32 pages $15

Hey, Dad, This is Belize!
This collection of vignettes of life in Belize was originally published in 1977; now in its 4th printing.   114 pages $12

Mexico

Choose Mexico
Retire on $800 a Month
Over 150,000 copies sold.   Precise instructions on where and how a couple can live on an income of $800 a month. Thousands of retirees now living in Mexico credit this book with showing them the way. 250 pages $14.95

Video Visits: Mexico
See the sunny beaches,   colorful towns, delicious foods and ancient ruins, that make Mexico the #1 haven for retirees. 53 minutes of magnificent color video VHS $29.95

RV Travel in Mexico
by John Howells. Directory of over 400 RV parks in Mexico.   Spanish terms for RV maintenance and repair. RV's and retirement in Mexico 228 pages $14.95

Mexico by Rail
by Gary A. Poole.
Learn how to plug into Mexico's remarkable and inexpensive rail network and enjoy leisurely, comfortable and terribly romantic travel by train. 350 pages $15.95

The People's Guide to Mexico
by Carl Franz
Everything you've wanted to know about Mexico, but were afraid to ask.   We think this should be required reading for anyone going to Mexico. This classic is now in its 10th edition!   608 pages $18.95

A Peoples Guide to Mexico Video
La Ruta Maya: River of Ruins
"Peoples Guide" authors Carl Franz and Lorena Havens take a small group way-off-the-beaten-path on an expedition from Tikal, Guatemala to Palenque, Mexico. Including 7 days on the Usumacinta River. Don't miss this one!.
32 Minutes $29.95

Mexico Reference Map
Entire country covered $10.95

Mexico South Map
Covers Guerrero and Oaxaca States and most of Puebla and Veracruz. Adjoins *Yucatan Map* to create larger map. $10.95

Cancun Handbook
by Chicki Mallan
A great guide if you plan to visit Belize, via Cancun. Lots of pictures and maps. 257 pages $14.95

Cancun Urban Area Map
Cozumel, Isla Mujeres, and Chetumal $9.95

Playas Caribe Map
Map of Mexico's Caribbean beaches, Cancun. Cozumel, Isla Mujeres $9.95

Pacific Mexico Handbook
By Bruce Whipperman. Mile by mile directions for exploring the 2,000 miles of gorgeous beaches and quite towns that so many North Americans are making their home. 428 pages $15.95

Playas Pacifico Map
Map of Mexico's Pacific Beaches with insets of Acapulco. Ixtapa and Zihuatanejo. $9.95

Yucatan Handbook
By Chicki Mallan
Outstanding guide to the Yucatan area.   Also has information on the surrounding states of Campeche, Tabasco and Quintana Roo.   395 pages $14.95

Yucatan Peninsula Map
Covers all of Mexican Yucatan, Belize and Eastern Guatemala.   Combines with the *Mexico South Map*. *$10.95*

Caribbean

Undiscovered Islands of the Caribbean
By Burl Willes
Gives details on 32 islands that have no big hotels and very few tourists.   Includes 6 islands of Belize.
262 pages $14.95

Video Visits: Islands of the Caribbean
Some of the most beautiful blue waters in the world. Deserted beaches. Rain-forests. Deserts and mountains. Sumptuous seafood. Reggae & Calypso. 53 Minutes $29.95

Blue Print For Paradise: How to Live on a Tropic Island
by Ross Norgrove
This book has everything you need to know about moving to and living comfortable in the tropics. Excellent information about designing and building a house. 202 pages $14.95

Retirement Handbooks

Retirement on a Shoestring
By John Howells
Simple strategies to make your retirement income go a lot farther.   How to live twice as well on social security.   The 50 best affordable retirement locations. 178 pages $14.95

Where to Retire
By John Howells. Your travel guide to America's best
places. An exhaustively researched directory of the best
places in the U.S. to retire, based on climate, cost of living,
housing. 372 pages $14.95

Get Up and Go
A Guide for the Mature Traveler
By Gene and Adele Malott
A directory of spectacular travel deals and discounts
available to people over 49. Valuable information for
younger travelers too. 325 pages $14.95

Adventures Abroad
Exploring the Travel Retirement Option
By Allene Symons and Jane Parker
Interviews with American retirees living in 17 different
foreign countries including: France, Italy, Spain, Portugal,
Greece, England, Ireland, Mexico, Costa Rica, Uruguay, the
Caribbean, and Thailand. 288 pages $14.95

Helpful Out-of-Print Books

Sorry to say these books are all out of print; try looking
for them in libraries and used book stores.

Gypsying After 40: A Guide to Adventure and Self
Discovery
by Robert W. Harris
The true story of an American couple who decided to leave
the rat race and see the world--on very little money. Great
tips on how to live comfortably and inexpensively, while
traveling abroad. One of our all time favorites. This book
is a real motivator!

How to Build Small Boats
By Edson I. Shock
Published by A.S.Barns N.Y., Copyright 1952

The People's Guide to R.V. Camping in Mexico
by Carl Franz
This book also includes a campground directory, describing many sites.

23 Boats You Can Build
By Popular Mechanics
Published by Popular Mechanics Press, Copyright 1950

Bill & Claire Gray's
Belize Retirement Tour

Over the years many of you have written and asked us to personally show you around Belize. You've finally succeeded in twisting our arm!

We've designed a Belize Retirement Tour specifically for our readers. This isn't standard tourist fare. We've planned a week long itinerary that will give you a sampling of what it's like to live in Belize. You'll travel throughout Belize meeting and visiting with North Americans who have made the move to Belize. We'll take you on a tour of available medical and dental facilities and also our favorite places to shop.

Another unique feature of our tour is its flexibility. The first week we guide you step by step, from the moment you arrive at the airport. After that, you can either fly home or stay up to another 3 weeks exploring on your own. You can spend a full month in Belize if you like.

The tour package will include round trip air-fare, hotel accommodations and some of your meals for the week, as well as all transportation within Belize. Are you interested? Write to us care of: *Preview Publishing, P.O. Box 1179, Pine Valley, CA 91962* and we'll send you more information.

Copper Bank fishing fleet repairing their boats, Corozal District

Glossary

Altun Ha: Mayan ruin from the Classic Period.

Ambergris: The most developed caye in Belize.

ATV: All terrain vehicle.

baboon: Creole word for monkey.

barrister: Lawyer.

Batty: Batty Brothers Bus Service.

BEL: Belize Electricity Limited   Formerly BEB.

Belizer: A Gringo who loves Belize.

Boledo: Belize lottery. From boleto, the Spanish word for ticket.

bridge: Dock; a wharf; a pier.

British Honduras: Name of Belize prior to independence.

BTL: Belize Telecommunications Limited.

bush: Jungle; thick forest.

Canero: Sugar cane truck driver; cane farmer or cutter.

Carib: Same as Garifuna; descendant of runaway African slave and Carib Indian; old Spanish name for cannibal.

Casa de Cambio: Money changing store.

caye, or cay: (Pronounced: KEY) Spanish word for small island.

cenote: Enormous natural well.

clearance letter: Police Certificate of Character.

collectivo: Collective taxi, usually a VW van.

conch: (Pronounced: KONK) Large spiral shelled marine mollusk; main ingredient of Conch soup.

Coolie: A Belizean of East Indian descent.

Creole: English dialect spoken in Belize; person of mixed ancestry.

escabeche: A spicy hot & sour chicken and onion soup.

Federales: Mexican Highway Patrol.

garnacha: Belizean tostada.

Garifuna: Same as Carib; African dialect spoken throughout the Caribbean.

Good-night!: Greeting used to mean "hello" after dark.

Gringo: North American; white person.

guava: Small tropical tree with sweet acidic fruit.

gunk-holeing: Sailing from one small harbor to the next.

habanero: Hottest chile pepper in the world!

Hindu: Belizean of East Indian descent.

jalapeno: Chile pepper.

Ketchi: Mayan dialect.

manatee: Sea Cow; aquatic mammal.

mangrove: Tropical maritime tree known for it's tangled mass of roots.

Maya: People and language of the ancient Yucatan and Belize.

Mennonites: German speaking sect; forerunners of the Amish; followers of Menno Simons.

Orange Walk: Orange plantation; name of town and district in N.Belize;

overhang: Roof projection that extends beyond the wall.

panada: Small deep fried fish pie.

P.G: Punta Gorda (literally "fat point"); town in S.Belize.

P.U.P: Peoples United Party.

Pesero: Money changer; one who buys pesos.

pipe water: Tap water.

plantain: Plant in banana family producing starchy fruits, used like a potato.

Quintana Roo: Mexican state bordering Belize.

Rasta: Religious sect; worshipers of Haile Selassie, who's real name was Ras Tafar.

Reggae: Rastafarian music, known for its syncopated beat.

salbute: Belizean tostada.

sapodilla: Fruit; tree used in production of chewing gum.

sapote: Mamey apple.

sugar cane: Chief cash crop of N. Belize.

toucan: Bird with very large brilliant colored beak; national bird of Belize.

tree chicken: Iguana; eaten during Lent.

U.D.P: United Democratic Party.

vat: Water cistern.

Venus: Bus line owned by the Gilharry Brothers.

walk: Orchard; plantation.

Xunantunich: Mayan ruin; tallest structure in Belize.

Yucatan: Geographical region north of Belize.

zericote: A hardwood prized by Belizean wood carvers for its swirls of chocolate brown color.

Index

ORDER HERE

TITLE	PRICE

	SUB TOTAL	
Check for RUSH ☐	SHIPPING	
	TAX	
	TOTAL	

NAME:

ADDRESS:

CITY: STATE: ZIP:

I authorize **Preview Publishing**
to charge my *Visa/MasterCard* number: MasterCard VISA

EXP. DATE:

Cardholder's
Name:

Cardholder's
Signature:

Preview Publishing, P.O. Box 1179
Pine Valley, CA 91962

ORDER HERE

TITLE	PRICE

	SUB TOTAL	
Check for RUSH ☐	SHIPPING	
	TAX	
	TOTAL	

NAME:

ADDRESS:

CITY: STATE: ZIP:

I authorize **Preview Publishing**
to charge my *Visa/MasterCard* number:

EXP. DATE:

Cardholder's
Name:

Cardholder's
Signature:

Preview Publishing, P.O. Box 1179
Pine Valley, CA 91962